Chicken Soup for the Teenage Soul's
The Real Deal: FRIENDS

Chicken Soup for the Teenage Soul's

The Real Deal:
FRIENDS

Best, Worst, Old, New, Lost, False, True and More

Jack Canfield
Mark Victor Hansen
Deborah Reber

Health Communications, Inc.
Deerfield Beach, Florida

www.hcibooks.com
www.chickensoup.com

Library of Congress Cataloging-in-Publication Data
is available from the Library of Congress.

Publisher: Health Communications, Inc.
         3201 S.W. 15th Street
         Deerfield Beach, FL 33442-8190

Cover and inside book design by Lawna Patterson Oldfield
Cover model: Cara Ann Higgins

CONTENTS

INTRODUCTION

FRIENDS. How important are they to *you?* If you're like most teens, friends are at the top of your list, and when you consider how much time you spend with them—whether hanging out by the lockers before school or Instant Messaging long after your parents have said "lights out"—it's no wonder that they have a huge influence on the person you are today.

Maybe that influence is a good thing. Maybe your friends push you to be a better person or help you get through difficult times in your personal life. Or maybe their influence isn't so great. Maybe your friends are the kind of people your parents would rather you didn't hang out with at all. And even though it's exciting being friends with the biggest rebel in school, when you're being honest with yourself, you'd have to agree with your mom and dad.

Friends can be our trusted confidants . . . our soft place to land . . . our Saturday night companions. And while friendships are not without challenges, they're usually worth it. There's nothing quite like the comfort that comes from knowing that someone's got your back when you need it most.

Have you had friends who've come and gone, and others who've stuck with you through thick and thin? Have you had nasty breakups with friends, where even though you didn't want it to happen, things ended up getting pretty ugly? Have you watched a friend go through something really tough and felt completely helpless? Have you been friends with someone of the opposite sex and then gotten confused when one of you started having feelings for the other?

Take comfort . . . you're not alone.

And that's why we decided to make this second book in the *Real Deal* series all about *friends*. Inside, you'll find *real* stories and poems from *real* teens—teens who write about their friendship highs and lows and everything in-between in the hope that their experiences might make a connection with you.

Once again, we received many, many more submissions than we could possibly include in this book, but we want to thank all of you who took the time to submit your poems and stories. Hats off to you! But even if we didn't include your story in this book, know that we did read each and every submission, and what you wrote let us know what issues were most important to you. We hope that you find your experiences reflected in this book.

Like the first book in the *Real Deal* series, this one is chock full of quizzes, side stories and tons of information on the kinds of things you want to know about: movies to see, books to read, fresh ways to look at tough situations, Web sites to check out and things to explore in your journal. Plus, this book also has my voice throughout. That's right . . . *me*. And while I'm not a teen anymore, I used to be one myself, and I continue working with teens today as a mentor and workshop leader. You'll get to know more about me in the introductions I've written to each story, especially since I lay it all on the line and tell it like it was and still is. Come to think of it, maybe I'm a bit too honest. In fact, my parents shouldn't read this book. *Hmmm* . . . I wonder if I'm too old to be grounded?

Oh, well . . . anyway, I hope you enjoy the book. And more than anything, I hope that it helps you to have more fulfilling relationships with the friends in your life today as well as all the friends you'll be collecting along the way.

Deborah Reber

ACKNOWLEDGMENTS

THE PATH TO *Chicken Soup for the Teenage Soul's The Real Deal: Friends* has been challenging and rewarding. Our heartfelt gratitude to:

Our families, who have been chicken soup for our souls!

Jack's family, Inga, Travis, Riley, Christopher, Oran and Kyle, for all their love and support.

Mark's family, Patty, Elisabeth and Melanie, for once again sharing and lovingly supporting us in creating another book.

Deborah's husband, Derin, and son, Asher, for sharing their love, energy and encouragement with us every day, as well as Dale, MaryLou and Michele Reber, and David and Barbara Basden for their ongoing support.

Our publisher, Peter Vegso, for his vision and commitment to bringing *Chicken Soup for the Soul* to the world.

Patty Aubery and Russ Kalmaski, for being there on every step of the journey, with love, laughter and endless creativity.

Barbara Lomonaco, for nourishing us with truly wonderful stories.

D'ette Corona, for her incredible powers of organization and securing all the permissions and bios for this book.

Patty Hansen, for her thorough and competent handling of the legal and licensing aspects of the *Chicken Soup for the Soul* books. You are magnificent at the challenge!

Laurie Hartman, for being a precious guardian of the *Chicken Soup* brand.

Veronica Romero, Teresa Esparza, Robin Yerian, Jesse Ianniello, Lauren Edelstein, Jody Emme, Debbie Lefever, Michelle Adams, Dee Dee Romanello, Shanna Vieyra, Lisa Williams, Gina Romanello, Brittany Shaw, Dena Jacobson, Tanya Jones and Mary McKay, who support Jack's and Mark's businesses with skill and love.

Bret Witter, Elisabeth Rinaldi, Allison Janse and Kathy Grant, our editors at Health Communications, Inc., for their devotion to excellence.

Terry Burke, Tom Sand, Lori Golden, Kelly Johnson Maragni, Patricia McConnell, Kim Weiss, Paola Fernandez-Rana, the marketing, sales, and PR departments at Health Communications, Inc., for doing such an incredible job supporting our books.

Tom Sand, Claude Choquette and Luc Jutras, who manage year after year to get our books translated into thirty-six languages around the world.

The art department at Health Communications, Inc., for their talent, creativity and unrelenting patience in producing book covers and inside designs that capture the essence of *Chicken Soup*: Larissa Hise Henoch, Lawna Patterson Oldfield, Andrea Perrine Brower, Anthony Clausi and Dawn Von Strolley Grove.

All the *Chicken Soup for the Soul* coauthors, who make it such a joy to be part of this *Chicken Soup* family.

Our readers who helped us make the final selections and made invaluable suggestions on how to improve the book, including Ed Adams, Daniel Barcott, Tipton Blish, Julie Johnson, AnneMarie Kane, Jamie Koelln, Bridget Perry, Renee Zak and Alice Wilder.

WriteGirl (*www.writegirl.org*), New Moon Publications (*www.newmoon.org*), Write On (*www.zest.net/writeon/*) and About Creative Writing for Teens (*teenwriting.about.com/*) for reaching out to teens everywhere in the search for submissions.

And, most of all, to everyone who submitted their heartfelt stories and poems for possible inclusion in this book. While we were not able to use everything you sent in, we know that each word came from a magical place flourishing within your soul.

Because of the size of this project, we may have left out the names of some people who contributed along the way. If so, we are sorry, but please know that we really do appreciate you very much.

We are truly grateful and love you all!

CHAPTER 1

WHAT IS A FRIEND?

What does friendship mean to you? When it comes to defining *friendship*, words like *loyalty* and *trust* come to mind. So do *honesty, reliability* and *respect*. Friends are the people who stick with us through thick and thin. The ones who see us at our very worst and don't think about us any differently. They know how to make us laugh and what to do when we cry. This chapter takes a look at what makes these special relationships so important in our lives.

WHEN I WAS ABOUT FOUR YEARS OLD, I got separated from my mom while grocery shopping. No doubt I wandered off to my favorite section—the Tasty Kakes aisle—and the next thing I knew, Mom was nowhere in sight. I became frantic. Eyes wide and heart racing, I starting rushing through the aisles in desperate search of my mom's capri pants, flowered blouse and signature horn-rimmed glasses.

The relief I felt when I finally spotted her was overwhelming. Life was good. Life would go on. Everything was as it should be. It's amazing how the very glimpse of someone familiar and loving can have such an incredible effect.

The First Day

The long hallway stretches before my feet. Lockers of royal blue line the walls. Unfamiliar faces dart in and out of the open doors, ignoring me. I shift my bag on my shoulder and look straight ahead.

I think I see a familiar face at the far end of the long hall. Unfortunately, the image passes by, and I cannot see the face any longer. The clock on the side of the wall blares the first bell. I frantically look for some sign of help. None is there.

I tuck my blonde hair behind my ear and straighten my jacket,

For Real?

It's true . . . there *are* more kids in high school! The average number of students in a **middle school** is **612**, while the average number in a **high school** is **753**.

trying to gain some form of confidence. Shakily, I pull my class schedule from my pocket. Searching over the wrinkled paper, I find the locker number printed in big bold letters: 131. Taking a deep breath, I shuffle into the hallway. The immediate rush of hot air mixed with cologne fills my nose, making it burn.

CONSIDER THIS . . .

A **locker** in school is the only place teens have for **stashing stuff** in **private** besides their bedrooms, so many **decorate** their lockers with pictures and art to make them **feel** more **like home**.

I look at the locker next to me: number 300. My locker will be at the other end of the hall. Sighing, I continue onward. A group of tall boys wearing honor jackets zooms by, their hair slicked back. As they strut past me, I continue to saunter down the never-ending hallway, trying to ignore them. A pair of gangster wannabes hits me in the shoulder. The taller one turns toward me as they walk away. He begins to chuckle to himself because he knows who I am. I'm the freshman.

HOW ABOUT YOU?

Have you ever dreamt that you **forgot** your **locker combination?**

Shaking it off, I stride past a group of senior girls. They are dabbing on the final touches of makeup and lip-gloss. I find myself laughing at their ditzy ways, wondering what drives them to be so . . . *pink?*

I'm more confident now as I pass locker number 200. I've seen so many different cliques by now that I know a little more of what to expect. But as I walk toward my destination,

Seen It?

In the movie *Broadcast News* (1987), Albert Brooks and Holly Hunter are such **close friends** they don't even have to **complete their sentences**. He tells her to "meet me at the place near the thing where we went that time," and **she knows exactly where he means**.

I find that I am missing something that all these people seem to have in common. They have somebody *with* them. And I am standing in the center of the high school hallway *alone.*

I dash past another group of students. My locker is now in sight. Shoving the bag inside locker 131, I search for someone I know. I see two kids from my classes last year. I wave, and they return the gesture, but without much enthusiasm, and continue to walk past me. Frantically, I search the passing faces, pleading for some sign of recognition.

I glance down the hall the same way I had come. There at the end I see them, all spread out and looking lost. I smile to myself as I see their worried faces. I notice my best friend is not with them and wonder where she could be. Not seeing her, I continue to wait for my lost friends to find their way to me. I begin to laugh out loud as a group of seniors strides by.

Consider This . . .

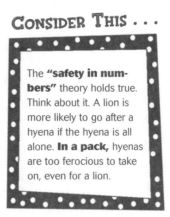

The **"safety in numbers"** theory holds true. Think about it. A lion is more likely to go after a hyena if the hyena is all alone. **In a pack,** hyenas are too ferocious to take on, even for a lion.

Address Book

If you're looking to make friends through an online community, check out the Student Center at *www.studentcenter.org*

Someone lightly taps my shoulder, and I turn to see who it is. My best friend stands there looking at me with amusement. I smile, relieved to see someone familiar. She laughs as I point to our lost friends, but she's not laughing at our friends; she's laughing at me. I ask her what's so funny, and she says simply, "I guarantee it, pal, you look much worse than they do."

I smile and have to agree. There are experiences in our lives that should be shared with other people, and the first day of school is one of them. I am grateful I have friends who can be with me through these adventures. That's what friends are for.

WHERE DO YOU STAND?

Are you all about your group of friends?

Answer the following "yes" or "no" questions to find out:

___ YES   You check your date book
___ NO   every week to make sure you
           don't miss anyone's birthday.

___ YES   You're somewhat of a pack-
___ NO   rat, refusing to get rid of any
           keepsakes from the times you
           and your friends spend
           together.

___ YES   Your list of IM buddies is
___ NO   longer than your parents'
           weekly grocery list.

___ YES   You feel practically naked if
___ NO   you walk down the hallway
           without at least one friend by
           your side.

___ YES   You regularly finish your best
___ NO   friend's sentences.

Clara Waddell, age 16

For Real?

When **Peeps**™ were first introduced in the 1920s, each one took **27 hours to make.** Compare that with today . . . **2 million** are **made every day!**

THE THEME SONG FROM *FRIENDS*. The smell of chocolate-chip cookies baking in an oven on a winter day. The soft white fur on my dog's ears. A package of slightly stale pink bunny Peeps™. For me, all of these things bring me comfort and happiness, not unlike a good friend. Of course, friends bring much more to us than a good laugh or warmth in our tummies, or even the ability to spur on a sugar-induced spaz attack. The author of the following poem thinks so, too. She's come up with the perfect recipe for a friend, and this is one recipe you won't find in *The Joy of Cooking*.

Read It?

The Joy of Cooking is one of the **most popular cookbooks** in the U.S., providing the know-how to make everything from meatloaf to crème brûlée.

Friendship Soup

Like tomato soup, only
Better, more
Satisfying, and
Good for your soul.
All you need is a can of love,
Opened with a smile,
Poured into a bowl of good
   environment and similar
   interests,
Mixed with: a

HOW ABOUT YOU?

If you were to write a recipe for the perfect friend, what would be *your* ingredients?

Cup of compliments,
3 cups of talking,
5 cups of time together—
House visits,
Two teaspoons of helpfulness,
Three trials of dependability,
(At least two "come-throughs"),
Shoulder cry-ons,
A gallon of hugs,
3 tons of encouragement,
Nix the envy,
And don't forget—a
Pinch of nuttiness.

Omenka Uchendu, age 14

For Real?

Long before Joseph Campbell (of Campbell Soup fame) shot tomato soup to popularity in 1897, **tomatoes** were **believed to be deadly poisonous!**

OUTSIDE THE BOX

So what makes up a good friend, anyway? Here are some things to look for when trying to find a new, good friend:

- Earns your trust. More than anything else, trust is tops when it comes to making a friend great.
- Shares some similar interests. You don't need to have everything in common ...just enough so that the two of you have fun hanging out.
- Likes you for who you are. There's nothing worse than feeling like you have to look or act a certain way when all you really want to do is kick back.
- Shares your value system. I'm not talking about politics here. I'm just saying that friends who share values and morals are more likely to get through challenges together.

ONE OF MY DEAREST FRIENDS LIVES 3,000 MILES AWAY. She's in New York City, and I'm in Seattle, so a lot of our communication takes place in the form of daily phone calls (thank God for cell phones with free long distance!), e-mails with lots of pics or IMing.

But nothing's better than stepping onto my front porch in my PJs to get the mail and finding an envelope with Alice's handwriting. Every now and then, my friend sends me things—a newspaper clipping she knew I'd find interesting, a little something she picked up for me while on a trip or photos from a recent vacation. And a package from Alice wouldn't be complete without a note telling me how much our friendship means to her and reminding me that she's thinking of me even though we can't meet at the corner Starbucks for a coffee later that day. I think I love these notes more than the contents of the package itself. It seems that no matter how many times she says it, I never get tired of hearing that I've got the love and support of a good friend.

HOW ABOUT YOU?

Have you ever written a note just to tell a friend how much you appreciate him or her?

Got a pile of photos, notes and other keepsakes and want to organize them so they're not holed up in a shoebox under the bed? Make a scrapbook! Here are some ideas for keeping the memories alive:

- Get creative! You can use all kinds of materials in your book—newspaper, fabric, stickers, pipe cleaners, burlap . . . the sky's the limit!
- Have fun with your photos . . . use wrapping paper or other colored paper for matting, or get out the scissors and cut them into cool shapes.
- Find keepsakes from your adventures together and stick them in. Ticket stubs, notes passed in class, programs from concerts, even receipts from 7-Eleven can jog the memories.
- Do some journaling in your scrapbook. Write about your friend and what you like to do together.

For more ideas, check out _The Complete Book of Scrapbooking: Projects and Techniques_ by Louise Riddell.

Dear Friend

Dear Friend,

I've known you since I first learned what the word "friend" means. We have always gone to the same schools, but have had only three years in the same class. I was always a little jealous of you. You were always more popular than I

WHERE DO YOU STAND?

Even the best of friends might get jealous of each other from time to time. Would you ever . . .

assume your friend cheated when he scored higher on a test than you?

___ NO WAY! (0 points)
___ MAYBE (1 point)
___ YEAH, PROBABLY (2 points)

want to find a boyfriend who was cuter than your BFF's guy?

___ NO WAY! (0 points)
___ MAYBE (1 point)
___ YEAH, PROBABLY (2 points)

wish you could afford to buy expensive designer clothes like your best friend?

___ NO WAY! (0 points)
___ MAYBE (1 point)
___ YEAH, PROBABLY (2 points)

go on a diet to try to get as skinny as your BFF?

___ NO WAY! (0 points)
___ MAYBE (1 point)
___ YEAH, PROBABLY (2 points)

be embarrassed that your parents drive a beat-up junker instead of a fancy SUV like your friend's folks?

___ NO WAY! (0 points)
___ MAYBE (1 point)
___ YEAH, PROBABLY (2 points)

Add up your points:
0–3 = Jealousy isn't a problem
4–6 = I'm only human
7–10 = I've got jealous tendencies

was, but that never meant that I wasn't right there with you. I've been there to hear about all of your crushes and all of the people who irritated you most. In fourth grade when you liked *him,* so did I. And when you got over it, I did, too. Even when you thought I hated you, I didn't. I thought it was you who hated me.

I was there when Emma wouldn't stop talking, and you were there when Nick was driving us crazy. I know your biggest secrets, and you know mine. Remember our little yellow notebook? I do.

I keep all of your notes and scraps of our friendship in a box, and when it's hard to believe that someone loves me, I pick through the slips of paper and pictures, thinking back to everything we've been through. I remember in preschool when you were the only one who could say my name right, and I remember when I kept spelling your name wrong.

I'll always love you, and I'll always remember you, even when I can't seem to make up my mind about anything else. And I'm writing this letter because I just wanted you to know.

Andja Budincich, age 13

HE KNOWS WHEN TO LISTEN. She knows when to speak. He knows when to give you a hug and when to give you some space. She knows that you love banana splits, but only with no bananas. Caesar salad? Dressing's gotta be on the side. He doesn't have to ask whether or not you want to hear music while you're studying together—he's already queued up your favorite song. She gives you the kind of good advice that only someone who can be completely honest with you would dare to give. He knows you well enough to be both your biggest critic and your biggest fan, all at the same time. Great friends can do it all.

Being a Friend

You're having a bad hair day or you have a huge zit and you just feel ugly.
The world stares at you.
A friend says, "You look hot!"

You get a bad grade on a test because you stayed up late doing a project for another class.
The world says, "You're a failure."
A friend says, "Good try, you'll do better next time."

Your crush doesn't give you the time of day.
The world flirts with them and leaves you brokenhearted.
A friend sets you up on a date with that person or says, "You can do better."

Your car breaks down in the middle of nowhere.
The world drives by.
A friend drives out to the middle of nowhere, picks you up and goes with you to the mechanic.

For Real?
Huge **zits** are more common than you might think! About **85%** of teens deal with **acne** at some point in their lives.

You don't have a date for prom night.
The world thinks you're a loser.
A friend sets you up with a cute cousin.

CONSIDER THIS . . .

Everybody trips now and then, even movie stars. While attending the London premiere of her movie *Miss Congeniality,* **Sandra Bullock** tripped on the red carpet and took a spill while photographers caught every second on film.

You slip on the wet grass and fall in a mud puddle.
The world laughs and walks on.
A friend laughs, then offers you a hand and hooks you up with a change of clothes.

Your loved one dies, you feel like you can't go on.
The world feels sorry for you.
A friend prays for you.

You feel fat and unhealthy.
The world thinks you should stop eating.
A friend jogs with you every day.

You want to die and are considering suicide.
The world ignores you and causes you more pain.
A friend gives you a reason to live.

Life's challenges cause you dismay.
The world forgets you.
A friend gives you love.

Rosie Ojeda, age 18

LISTEN TO THE LYRICS OF SOME OF YOUR FAVORITE SONGS. Chances are, they are full of metaphors or symbols that represent other words. Take Nelly Furtado's song "I'm Like a Bird." She likens herself to a bird because just writing about the fact that she's doesn't stick around when her heart is involved might not sound as poetic or as powerful. Sometimes feelings and emotions are so intense that simple words and descriptions don't do them justice. The author of this next poem has found a way to express his relationship with his close friend by using a clever metaphor.

Read It?

Sarah Dressen's novel *Someone Like You* tells the story of best friends Halley and Scarlett as they turn to each other to deal with their separate hardships.

The Gardener

I call my friend the Gardener
For many reasons.
Reasons that start to coil around me,
Enveloping me,
Making me feel secure.

The Gardener has been there
Since I was a seed.
Helping water me with love,
Protecting me from the weeds in my life.

All of my best friends are gardeners.
I consider myself a gardener, too,

By helping my friends grow,
By caring for them,
And weeding out their troubles.

Everyone can be a gardener by
    tending to their friends.
As they grow in life, you will
    also grow.

Joel Kristenson, age 15

For Real?
Would it **surprise** you to
know that **45** minutes
of gardening **burns** as
many **calories** as
30 minutes of aerobics?

OUTSIDE THE BOX

The word <u>gardener</u> is a <u>metaphor</u> or symbol for
"friend" in this poem. Can you think of any metaphors
for the friends in your life? If you're up for a
little journaling, try seeing if your friends fit into
any of these metaphors. Write about how they
might be compared with a:

- mirror
- glass of juice
- constellation
- comforter or pillow
- good book

For example, I have a friend who's just like a
mirror . . . she reflects back my best qualities,
and she never lies.

Take the Quiz:
DO YOU KNOW WHAT A FRIEND IS

1. It's the first day of school, and you're embarrassed to see that your best friend is wearing a dorky outfit. To make matters worse, a popular group of older kids has noticed your friend's lack of style and is making fun of you both while you're minding your own business in the cafeteria. You . . .

 ___ A. are among the most loyal people you know, and today is no different. You stick up for your friend, no matter how badly it might affect your rep for the next three years.

 ___ B. grab your friend's arm and drag her away, red-faced with embarrassment. You plan to talk with her on the phone that night about making better fashion choices in the future.

 ___ C. pretend to get a cell-phone call and step aside to answer it so the popular group won't see you're with your friend. There's no way you want to start off at a new school like this.

2. You and your best friend have been looking forward to the spring dance for months, and you're planning to go stag together. But the week before the big event, she breaks her leg playing field hockey and is laid up at home in a cast. She is devastated to miss out on the dance. You . . .

 ___ A. grab your favorite DVDs, a box of microwave popcorn and your sleeping bag. The dance won't be the same without her, and you know how much a sleepover would mean to her.

 ___ B. are torn about what to do, and eventually end up compromising by making a brief appearance at the dance before heading over to your friend's house to keep her company.

___ C. decide to go to the dance anyway, figuring that your friend would do the same if the roles were reversed. After all, it's only one night, and you can make it up to her another time.

3. Your friend calls you right smack in the middle of the final episode of *American Idol* and wants to talk. He just found out that the girl he worships is interested in another guy and is devastated. You . . .

___ A. can tell by the sound of his voice that if you don't talk to him now, he might spiral into depression, so you turn off the boob tube and talk it out with him. You can always find out who won on Yahoo later on.

___ B. lower the volume on the TV and half-watch the program while half-listening to your friend. He really just needs to talk it out anyway . . . you're just a sounding board. He won't even know that you're not "all there."

___ C. pretend that your dad is on the other line, and ask him if you can call him back later. Hey, an hour or two won't make a difference in the long run, right?

4. You notice your best friend has been acting kind of differently ever since starting high school. She's dressing differently, purposefully dumbing herself down and has dropped out of the after-school sports you used to do together. You . . .

___ A. want to respect your friend's ability to make her own decisions, but feel strongly that you need to at least let her know that you're concerned about her, so you check in and see if there's anything wrong.

___ B. let it slide for now. If she wants to change, that's her business. As long as she isn't doing anything illegal, there's no point in ruffling any feathers.

___ C. take it personally that she's acting so differently, figuring that she must be mad at you. Well, two can play at that game . . . if she's going to be all weird, then so will you.

5. Your best friend has just gotten dumped by a guy she's crushed on forever. Even though they dated only a few times, and you think he's kind of a jerk in the first place, you know that your friend was head over heels in love with him. The thing is, he's all she's been talking about for years. You . . .

    ___ A. spend hours on the phone listening to your friend and giving her a shoulder to cry on. You might not understand what she liked about him in the first place, but her feelings are genuine, and you are sensitive to them.

    ___ B. try to comfort your friend when it initially happens, but lose patience when she's still harping over the loss of this guy a week later. Can't she see that he was completely wrong for her?

    ___ C. cut her off whenever she wants to go into it. You're so relieved that she's no longer dating this loser that you can't bear to hear about him for one more second!

So, how'd you do? Give yourself 10 points for every A, 20 points for every B and 30 points for every C. Do you know what a friend is?

50–70 points = You could write the textbook to Friendship 101. You know that the criteria for a good friend is trust, loyalty and reliability, and you're full of all three.

80–120 points = You know what a friend is most of the time, but occasionally find yourself in situations where you're not sure how a true friend would act. Your intentions are right on; now it's time to be a little more sensitive to your friends' needs.

130–150 points = You might want to study up on how to be a better friend since most of the time you're only thinking of yourself. Friendships are relationships full of *give* and take, not *take* and take. Try to find more balance.

CHAPTER 2

FRIENDSHIP CHALLENGES

M aking friends isn't always easy, and gathering up the courage to let people in can be tough. And once we have friends, things aren't always smooth sailing. So what do we do when shyness paralyzes us whenever potential friends are near? How should we act when a friend crosses a line and pushes us too far? This chapter explores some of the many challenges that we face among friends.

NO MATTER HOW HOT IT IS IN THE BRUTAL SUN OF AUGUST, I will stand on the edge of the swimming pool too scared to jump in. The plastic lounge chairs around the pool could be melting into piles of green and white goop on the cement, and I'd still stand there, frozen at the thought of how the cold water will shock my system.

What's up with that? I've done it before, and it's never killed me. In fact, it's never as bad as I think it's going to be, and the payoff is always worth it. It's the same with making new friends. Sometimes taking the plunge and exposing yourself to others can be paralyzing, but if you leap right in, feet first, you'll almost always be rewarded with a friendship.

Crossing the Fence

Mommy, can I eat lunch with you in your car?"

A pained look fell on my mom's face, but only for a second, as she said, "Of course, dear." As I ate my sub sandwich and drank my juice, she must have looked at me with sorrow in her heart—nobody wants her child to be lonely. I didn't even know that she had seen me circling the field moments ago, squishing the grass by myself, the lone little black girl with beautiful braids coiled and dormant under her rain hat, cowering from the wind and from people.

CONSIDER THIS . . .

Sub sandwiches, which are any long sandwich containing meat, cheese and condiments, are **also known as** Dagwoods, hoagies, grinders, heroes and po' boys.

Lunch recess in first grade was always sheer torture. To my shy, timid eyes, the children at the new school I had just moved to were leering at me, faces full of lechery. Scared and frightened and helplessly anti-social, I strayed away, pulled back from the curious and kind eyes, too afraid to speak up and out, too afraid of possible rejection from all the nice little white kids my own age. I was just over six years old, and my best friend was a fence.

The stick clanged as it bumped along the chain-link fence surrounding the elementary-school playground. Wood hit metal as I trailed the fenced perimeter of the field, stick in my right hand and hunger in my left. My mommy was going to drop off my lunch at school that day, and she hadn't come yet. So, clad in my orange raincoat, hat and big rubber boots, I kept my head down and roamed, friendless and sad.

The winds toyed with the tears in my eyes. *Even the air is popular,* I thought. *If only people liked me. If only I weren't so quiet and boring and stupid. If only I were pretty and long-haired like Amy. Maybe then I would have friends,* I cried to myself. Suddenly, my fingers seemed very interesting to me, and, having nothing else to do, I studied them, noting the loops and swirls and hoops that God had imprinted on them. Then I noticed our family's huge maroon Aerostar van swooping in across the field in the parking lot. Mom was here. I ran with hunched shoulders, the wind at my back and water lurching up

For Real?

While dogs and cats don't have **fingerprints**, primates, like **monkeys** and **gorillas**, do. And just like human **fingerprints**, each one is unique.

HOW ABOUT YOU?

Have you ever **struggled** with **shyness?** How did you handle it?

from under my rubbers. Breathless, I reached the car and slapped the front passenger door. Mom opened it.

"Hi, baby! How are you?"

"Good," I said, even though that was the farthest thing from the truth.

Mom handed me my lunch in a nice purple lunchbox as I leaned over the passenger seat talking to her. It stayed in her hand, floating in midair. Was I really going to take it and sit against the wall by myself eating, watching all the other kids play tag and ring-around-the-rosy? Self-conscious? Friendless? I looked at the purple lunchbox and then into my mom's eyes. I can only imagine what she saw in mine.

"Do you want to . . ." she said.

"Mommy, can I . . ." I said.

We both spoke at the same time.

"Go ahead, Meme," she said, letting me go first. I then asked her the question that summed up the sad fact of my social life.

"Can I eat lunch in the car?"

How to make friends was a lesson my own mother had to learn, as well. Fortunately, I learned it by the age of eight. By then I had a whole band of friends. I guess I finally realized that to be a friend to someone else, I would have to be a friend to myself. There was no way a

Seen It?

In *My Big Fat Greek Wedding* (2002), Toula gets so shy she hides behind the counter at her family's diner.

person would want to be friends
with me when I was hiding from the
world within a shroud of shyness.
So I learned to throw off that shroud
and let my inner self shine. I also
learned that friendships are made
only by communication, that the only

Address Book

Are you struggling with
shyness? A great place to
turn for help is Shake
Your Shyness at
www.shakeyourshyness.com

way someone would know I wanted to be her friend was if I
spoke up. "Hi!" and "Would you like to play with me?" became
my new catch phrases. Finally, I wasn't alone anymore.

Now, at the age of fourteen, I look back on most of my
friendships and realize that they are ones that I instigated.
Considering my early childhood, it's ironic that now I am the
one who reaches out to the people around me. I'm the one
who warms another's day with a random act of kindness and
watches a friendship bloom. I'm the one who chooses to open
up and share some of myself, making a bond with someone
else who opened up to me.

As I matured, I learned to cross the fence. I challenge
everyone, whether shy or bold, to cross the fence from the
side of shyness and pride or even hate, to the side of humil-
ity and warmth and love, to friendships that can last a long
time. To cross the fence instead of trailing it.

Omenka Uchendu, age 14

Spotlight On... SHYNESS

Most people feel shy at some point in their lives, but for others, shyness is a way of life. People who are shy tend to be uncomfortable in social situations. People with extreme shyness might not be able to deal with what others would find simple tasks, like standing up in front of the class or introducing themselves to someone new . . . even ordering a burger from a fast-food joint.

Shyness isn't rare either. Fifty percent of the population is shy on some level . . . even these famous celebrities: Barbara Walters, Henry Fonda, Sigourney Weaver and Nicole Kidman.

But don't wory . . . even if you're shy, there are ways to overcome it. Here are some tips:

- Plan ahead what you're going to say or how you'll handle social situations. Practice and role play to feel more comfortable.
- Let your friends and family know that you're shy so they can be sensitive to your feelings in potentially scary situations.
- When in a new situation, don't focus on yourself so much. Put your energy into learning about others and not on what others might be thinking of you.

- If you're scared of what might happen, try to imagine the worst-case scenario and then ask yourself this question: Is it really that bad?
- Be patient . . . don't expect to overcome your shyness immediately.

I WAS FLIPPING THROUGH MY SENIOR-CLASS YEARBOOK the other day and slowly paged through the photos of my classmates. I went to a pretty small school—my grade had only 130 kids or so in it—so I figured I would know everyone. I couldn't believe that there were at least a dozen kids on the glossy pages that I don't remember ever talking to, let alone seeing during the changing of classes or standing in line in the caf.

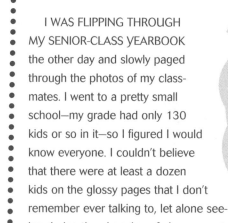

For Real?
The **first yearbooks** were created in the **1600s**. Back then, they were books for keeping written notes and school memorabilia, since photos weren't around yet.

How could I have missed them? Was I too busy to notice them, or were they too busy with the work of trying to blend in and not being noticed? Probably a little bit of both. I won the senior class award for being the Most Outspoken (actually I tied for the award with my BFF), so blending in wasn't something I was, or am, really familiar with. The author of this next story shares what it's like to be invisible.

Seen It?

The dark comedy *Ghost World* (2000), based on the comic book by Daniel Clowes, tells the story of best friends Enid and Rebecca, who are **social outsiders**.

A Volunteer from the Audience

I wasn't really the attention-demanding type. In fact, I would say I was rather quiet and shy. And because of my shy disposition, I was often ignored or simply forgotten about. Most of the time, I was left out of conversations or shuffled from class to class all alone. It's not that I avoided people—I just didn't try to be a part of activities. I guess I felt that if things were supposed to be, then they would happen, and I didn't really have much control over that.

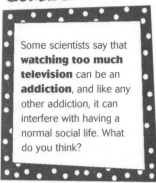

CONSIDER THIS . . .

Some scientists say that **watching too much television** can be an **addiction**, and like any other addiction, it can interfere with having a normal social life. What do you think?

I liked to watch people, though. I watched their laughter and their sorrows and the complications that followed them throughout the day—it was very much like watching television. I was just never a part of it. I was the audience, clapping for the comedians and booing the villains. And that was pretty much my social life.

Knowing now that I was more a part of the background than a part of society, you can understand why a small thing touched me so deeply. Any act of kindness by a stranger was wonderful in my mind . . . a pleasant reminder that I had not faded away from the world and that others could indeed see

For Real?

The average person takes between **3,000** and **6,000 steps every day**. Two thousand steps equal a mile for most people. How many steps do you think you walk in a day?

me. A pleasant reminder I was not a ghost, floating aimlessly in a corner.

This particular act of kindness took place one afternoon at school. My last class was math, and I had to walk all the way from the north side of the school to the south side, which might not seem like a big deal, but was challenging when one has only four minutes between classes and even fewer when a teacher keeps a class late. So there I was, feeling sweaty and tired and utterly unpopular, when I arrived at math class. And who was coming to the classroom door at the same time but one of the guys I liked to watch in my third-period class. Laugh at me all you want, but I'm the kind of person to run away from someone I don't know all that well. I'm too afraid of rejection. But this guy reached the door before me, and instead of just going inside, he held it open for me and said, "After you."

This was *huge* to me. Not only was someone actually noticing me, talking to me and opening doors for me, but also it was someone well-liked among my classmates. Someone who could easily ruin a reputation, *his reputation,* just by being seen with me. Yet there he was, actually being polite and, dare I say it, *nice* to me.

I walked into class, sat down in

THE WORD

Some say that **chivalry,** or courtesy and honor toward women (like when a guy holds a door open for a girl), **is dead.** What do you think? Should guys be chivalrous to girls?

CONSIDER THIS . . .

The **Girl Scouts** of America recently launched a campaign called **Girls Go Tech** to encourage more girls to focus on **math, science** and **technology**—areas of study that are typically dominated by boys.

WHERE DO YOU STAND?

Do you do things just to be a part of the crowd? Would you ever . . .

lie about acing the big test because being smart isn't cool?

___ NOPE, NOT ME   (0 points)
___ EVERY NOW AND THEN   (1 point)
___ YEAH, SO WHAT?   (2 points)

blow your entire month's allowance on a pair of jeans because they were the only ones to be seen in?

___ NOPE, NOT ME   (0 points)
___ EVERY NOW AND THEN   (1 point)
___ YEAH, SO WHAT?   (2 points)

program in the phone numbers of the coolest kids in school into your cell phone even though you never use them?

___ NOPE, NOT ME   (0 points)
___ EVERY NOW AND THEN   (1 point)
___ YEAH, SO WHAT?   (2 points)

complain about your parents to a friend just to sympathize with her even when you don't believe what you're saying?

___ NOPE, NOT ME   (0 points)
___ EVERY NOW AND THEN   (1 point)
___ YEAH, SO WHAT?   (2 points)

blow off the spring dance because your new group of friends think the dance is for losers?

___ NOPE, NOT ME   (0 points)
___ EVERY NOW AND THEN   (1 point)
___ YEAH, SO WHAT?   (2 points)

Add up your points:
0–3 = I can be a follower
4–7 = Depends on my mood
8–10 = I march to my own drum

my seat, and proceeded to pull out my notebook and complete the warm-up on the board. I love numbers and all you can do with them . . . nice, straight lines and rigid rules, no exceptions. But maybe the rules for social outcasts change from time to time.

I've actually made more friends since that day. Not loads, but the ones I have are extremely close. And though that act of kindness was not solely responsible for my late social bloom, it helped me be less afraid of what others would think of me if I did put myself out there. It helped me to be less afraid to botch up my lines when I finally stopped watching television and took part in the show. I have yet to overcome my social anxiety, but if someone popular and kind could see the ghost of an insecure outcast, maybe there is a way to be a part of the world and not just a part of the background.

Veronica Engler, age 14

🌳

THIS GIRL AT MY HIGH SCHOOL WENT HOME one Friday afternoon a quiet, nondescript student and came in the following Monday morning labeled a slut. The stories of what she had done at a party over the weekend were swirling around my school like a tornado. Being inexperienced and naïve, I remember joining my friends in thinking the gossip must be true. In no time, her new reputation was sealed in stone, and within a few months she abruptly left school, never to return.

Today, I'm still filled with embarrassment and shame that I didn't reach out to this girl when it all went down, that I chose to believe the gossip instead of examining the situation from a different perspective. If I could do it all over again, I would stand up for her. I would do my part to stop the rumors. I would let her know I was on her side. I would be her friend.

CONSIDER THIS . . .

The **emotional effects** of being labeled a **slut** can last long into adulthood. Sometimes when people repeatedly say things about someone, **they start to believe they're true**.

Not Really a Friend

For as long as I've known Naicia, I've known that she was one of the unpopular people in school. It was easy to tell, of course. Kids made it clear every single day. Naicia's peers jeered and called her horrible names, saying hurtful things like, "Hey, watch out guys! The whale is coming! Look at all that blubber!" This continued throughout elementary and into middle school.

Read It?

Linda, the main character in Judy Blume's classic, *Blubber,* takes the brunt of **teasing** by her classmates because she is **overweight**.

I used to be mystified at how strong Naicia seemed in the face of her tormentors. She would always stand up to them, even at the risk of getting detention or in-school suspension. It seemed like Naicia didn't let the cruel things that people said get to her, and for that I admired her from afar and still do. I wasn't one of the many taunting students in the hall, shouting out swear words. I listened to her, no matter what she had to say, but I still didn't consider her to be a "friend," and I'm not sure why.

CONSIDER THIS . . .

It's probably no surprise, but girls with **higher self-esteem** are much more likely to **abstain** from **sex** than those with low self-esteem.

Peer pressure is a horrible thing. It changes a person.

One day I was walking from science class to the cafeteria where I was hoping to find my favorite lunch: pizza. On the way I had to stop at my locker to drop off my notebook and pick up my wallet and ID card.

"Hey, Tawner!" I heard someone call from behind me.

Seen It?

Mean Girls (2004) features a classic lunchroom scene where the hierarchy of the student body is crystal clear.

"Oh, hey, Naicia," I responded without even turning around. There was only one person in the world who called me "Tawner."

"Ooh, guess what! I'm going out with Marcus again . . ."

"Not now, it's lunch. Tell me later or something," I replied, cutting her off. I was tired and in one of my less peppy moods, and I really didn't feel like hearing the latest updates on Naicia's strange love life.

"Okay!" she said brightly and wandered off.

I walked into the cafeteria and saw the usual groups and cliques, and headed for line number three, my line of choice even though it's usually the slowest one out of all five. I got my pepperoni pizza, fries and a brownie (talk about healthier foods in schools today?

CONSIDER THIS . . .

In 2002, the Los Angeles Unified School District dealt a **major blow** to the **junk-food** industry by **banning soda** machines on school grounds.

Yeah, right) and sat down with my core group of friends.

For Real?

Poor nutrition is a major factor in the increase of Type 2 **diabetes**. In fact, **45%** of new cases diagnosed each year are among **kids** under nineteen years old.

I'm sad to say that the friends who had made it through my intensive screening process were among the tormentors who tortured Naicia every day. And I'm even sadder to say (and rather disgusted as well) that I didn't even stick up for Naicia when my own friends put her down that day. Where was the logic in that? I was too afraid to stand up for what I believed in because I knew it would put my reputation at risk.

I now know that my reputation doesn't matter—the feelings of another human being do. For someone to purposely put someone else down and shatter her sense of self is one of the most horrible things a person can do.

Naicia wasn't as strong as I thought she was when we were in elementary school. She dealt with the pressures of being teased and tormented each day by trying to grow up before she was ready. Naicia's boyfriends changed as rapidly as the days of the week. The rumors that she does drugs aren't entirely false. Her mother wasn't exactly what you'd call a positive influence. It turns out that what I had thought were signs of strength were actually signs of someone who didn't know where to turn. So Naicia turned to drugs, sex and violence. She thought it was the only alternative.

Read It?

Real Girl Real World (2005) by Heather Gray and Samantha Phillips gives insight into the way **bad reputations** in school can affect the kids they're dumped on.

My experiences with Naicia have made me realize something about myself that I don't like, but luckily it's something I can change. Naicia still hangs around with the wrong crowd, still experiments with drugs and still has a tense home life, and I know I can't change any of that. But what I *can* change is how I treat others because the Golden Rule—treat others how you would like to be treated—still applies. I think everyone should live by that mantra.

I start high school next year. Naicia made it through, too, even with her poor grades. I have promised myself with the writing of this that I will change myself. I will see others as people who are thinking and feeling . . . people who have emotions . . . people who are just like me. And this time I will not be someone who just talks to Naicia because no one else has a kind thing to say to her. I'll do it because I'm her friend.

Tawnee Calhoun, age 15

Spotlight On . . . GETTING A BAD REPUTATION

Labels, gossip and rumors can all contribute to getting stuck with a bad reputation, whether or not it's deserved. And having a bad reputation can be extremely difficult to deal with, leading to depression and lowered self-esteem. Sometimes the targets of gossip and rumors are so affected by their reputations that they choose to drop out of school and try to start fresh somewhere else. So what can you do if you've gotten a bad reputation and you want to wipe the slate clean?

- Stand up for yourself! If people say or do things to reinforce the negative reputation, let them know it just ain't so, and surround yourself with friends who'll do the same.

- It's never too late to make a change. Even if you've acted in a way that reinforces the bad reputation, make a fresh start and stick with it!
- You can't force people to change the way they think about you. The best way to get others to respect you is to respect yourself.
- Give it some time. Don't expect people to notice the new you and change their minds right away.
- Get help from an adult. Sometimes bad reputations become too big of a problem to handle yourself. Turn to parents or teachers if you need some intervention.

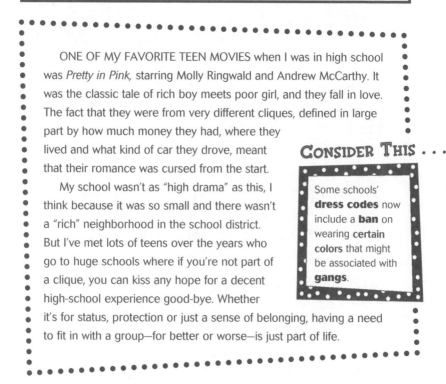

ONE OF MY FAVORITE TEEN MOVIES when I was in high school was *Pretty in Pink,* starring Molly Ringwald and Andrew McCarthy. It was the classic tale of rich boy meets poor girl, and they fall in love. The fact that they were from very different cliques, defined in large part by how much money they had, where they lived and what kind of car they drove, meant that their romance was cursed from the start.

CONSIDER THIS . . .

Some schools' **dress codes** now include a **ban** on wearing **certain colors** that might be associated with **gangs**.

My school wasn't as "high drama" as this, I think because it was so small and there wasn't a "rich" neighborhood in the school district. But I've met lots of teens over the years who go to huge schools where if you're not part of a clique, you can kiss any hope for a decent high-school experience good-bye. Whether it's for status, protection or just a sense of belonging, having a need to fit in with a group—for better or worse—is just part of life.

The In-Crowd

W hen I was in eighth grade, everyone was judged by his or her social status. I happened to be part of the outcasts, who really didn't care which rank they were placed in. I just wanted to live my life without having to worry about fitting into any superficial cliques like the "C-Town" group. It sounds ridiculously absurd to me now, but back then, if you weren't part of the "C-Town" crew, you didn't matter. If you were lucky and had "C-Town" friends, fitting into the group would be a breeze.

My own group of friends consisted of three of my P.E. teammates. We had connected on many levels, sharing laughter, tears, anger and hopes. It felt great having people in my life who cared about the real me. Or so I thought.

One day, one of my friends asked to speak with me privately. I was secretly envious of her, mostly because of her natural beauty. That day she told me that she was really glad to have me as a friend and that I was a really nice person. I was overwhelmed until she informed me that if I wanted to continue being her friend, I'd have to improve my appearance so I'd be pretty enough to hang out with her group. After shedding some tears, I finally regained my strength and decided to search for another group to join because I realized that those girls weren't true friends.

For Real?

Girls feel a **ton of pressure** to be **pretty**, especially because the images they see on TV and in the movies aren't realistic. In fact, two-thirds of girls say they aspire to look like a character on TV.

Since my social status was in the lower rank, it was harder to find a group. I finally decided to hang out with the "K-Rockers." Though their interests were exceedingly different from mine, they welcomed me into their group. Soon, I was constantly

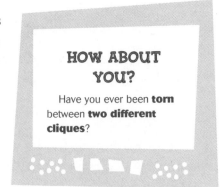

HOW ABOUT YOU?

Have you ever been **torn** between **two different cliques**?

being tempted to try drugs, and my concentration on my studies was diminishing. Though I never did try drugs, I was uncomfortable being around people who did. I wanted to leave the group because I knew they were negative influences, but I still hung out with them while keeping an eye out for another group to join.

Eventually, I met two girls in my P.E. class who were very pleasant to me. We talked every day during class until I finally asked them where they hung out. To my surprise, they were part of the "C-Town" group. I decided that if these nice girls were part of "C-Town," then I had misjudged the group the whole time. Maybe they weren't so bad after all. They accepted me immediately into their group. I never knew I would have "C-Town" connections, and it actually made me feel special.

It shouldn't have been a big deal, but for some reason I suddenly felt incredibly important. The first day with the "C-Town" group was really entertaining. I kept close with four girls. I loved hanging with the group because we had so much fun gossiping about people and talking about boys. Soon, more people started noticing me, and day by day, my popularity rank increased. Everything seemed perfect.

Then one day, one of the girls decided it would be funny to kick me out of the group just to mess with me. I ended up sobbing over a mean, practical joke. I recovered quickly, but every day the jokes increased. It seemed as if I was the only one she liked to pick on. It was annoyingly repetitive, and the jokes got so harsh that I began crying after each one.

"It was just a joke, Tiffany. Don't be such a baby," she'd say.

Then one day, she went too far and turned all the other girls against me. She pretended that she wanted to rumble with me, and after discovering it was another joke, it not only irritated me,

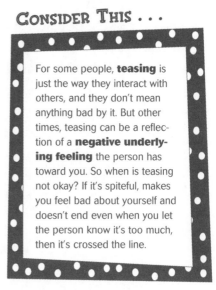

CONSIDER THIS . . .

For some people, **teasing** is just the way they interact with others, and they don't mean anything bad by it. But other times, teasing can be a reflection of a **negative underlying feeling** the person has toward you. So when is teasing not okay? If it's spiteful, makes you feel bad about yourself and doesn't end even when you let the person know it's too much, then it's crossed the line.

but also permanently angered me. I suddenly decided to stop hanging out with the "C-Town" girls and joined another group.

The girl apologized and told me I had to learn how to accept jokes. I explained to her that if she was a real friend, she would understand me, instead of poking fun at me for her own sick amusement. After my last words, we all ignored each other. Apparently, leaving "C-Town" was a huge mistake. Not only did I lose my hangout, but I had gained my first set of enemies. The girls all attempted to make my life miserable. They tried to get the entire school to dislike me and sent me threatening letters. Life was very depressing. This continued through junior year.

By the time senior year came, I was a completely changed person. I learned how to tolerate the "C-Town" girls. I made new friends, and with time, patience and a stronger mind, everything was finally okay.

I used to think that being popular was the most important thing. I would cry almost every night, wondering why I was so disliked. Now, I'm glad I went through such hardships, because I am a much stronger person, and the experience prepared me for the future. It taught me to be my own person and not to depend on others. I don't need to prove myself by hanging out with popular people. I've lost my naïveté and gained a more logical point of view. Now, I'm doing great in school, I have a lot of wonderful friends, and I have a stronger intellect. Due to all the past mishaps, I've matured greatly and, hopefully, the "C-Town" girls have, too.

Tiffany Cheng, age 18

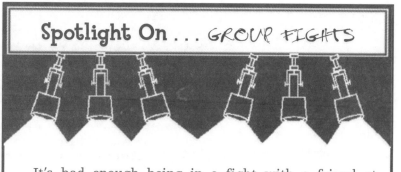

Spotlight On . . . GROUP FIGHTS

It's bad enough being in a fight with a friend at school, but when other friends get sucked into the drama, things can go from bad to worse in no time. Depending on who you're fighting with and what it's about, sometimes other friends feel the need to take sides, which just escalates the problem and makes it harder to resolve. While you can't control what other people do, here are a few ways to make sure that you don't contribute to any group fights:

- If you're having problems with a friend, try not to get other people involved and try to resolve the conflict yourself.
- If a friend starts bad-mouthing another friend in front of you, refuse to get sucked in.
- Don't believe anything you hear until you know it's true. Friends who are fighting are prone to spread untrue gossip and rumors.
- Even if the person you're fighting with has gotten others involved, don't stoop to their level. Group fights rarely end well for anybody, and if you hold your head high and act with dignity, you'll come out on top in the end.

I ALWAYS KNEW THERE WAS SOMETHING SLIGHTLY DANGEROUS about my friendship with Samantha. I knew that even though I was drawn to her like a moth to a flame, if I got too close I'd get my wings singed, or worse. There were lots of warning signs that the friendship wasn't so healthy. Sometimes she'd make fun of me to the point where it just didn't feel like *fun* anymore. I never felt like she had my back when I had no one else to turn to. And there were things about Sam's values that went against who I was at my very core.

I put up with a lot from Samantha (although I'm not quite sure why), but finally one night, I decided I couldn't take anymore. At a New Year's Eve party, my friend started ragging on me for hanging out with this other friend, Dan, whom she didn't approve of. She used all kinds of racial slurs while she was at it.

WHERE DO YOU STAND?

What's crossing the line for you when it comes to acceptable behavior in a friendship? Check the things below that you think are going too far:

❏ Going behind your back to another friend

❏ Cheating off you on a test

❏ Not standing up for you when confronted by bullies

❏ Not telling you about an online rumor going around about you

❏ Bad-mouthing your sister or brother to another friend

❏ Teasing you and saying you're too sensitive when you get upset

❏ Jumping to conclusions and accusing you of something you didn't do

❏ Reading your journal after you left it behind at a sleepover

❏ Going after a boy or girl that you like

❏ Stealing the spotlight from you at a party in your honor

My spirits plummeted, along with my jaw, which was now dropped to the floor. Suddenly, it was crystal clear to me that the differences between Samantha and I were a chasm too huge to overcome. (An image of the Grand Canyon comes to mind.)

I spent the next hour at the party defending Dan to Samantha, and trying to show Samantha just how unbelievably wrong she was about the things she was saying. But I finally realized there was no point.

More things than the year 1997 ended that night. My friendship with Samantha was over. I remember feeling a sense of relief. And even though I still look back on that friendship and wonder why I waited so long to get out of it, I'm glad I finally realized that some lines just can't be crossed.

A Deck of Snails

When I was thirteen years old, my parents took me to an art exhibit in England, where we were traveling. I was completely exhausted, and my expectations for the art exhibit were less than high. But once at the museum, I soon realized just how wrong I was. The vivacity of Salvador Dali cannot be put into words. My dad explained to me how unique Dali was, that no one else at the time was depicting what they *thought* as opposed to what they *saw* in their art. I've since

For Real?

The exact origin of **Solitaire** (card games that are for one player only) is unknown, but it has been around for at least **700 years**!

come to believe that everything in life has a corresponding metaphor.

For Jacob, that metaphor is Solitaire. I cannot even see his face in my mind—only his eyes. He has the most extraordinary eyes with solid, deep amber, unchanging irises. Sometimes when we talked, I wouldn't even hear a word he said. I was too busy being entranced by his eyes.

CONSIDER THIS · · ·

Spanish artist Salvador Dali, whose most famous **painting** is called "The Persistence of Memory," actually used **Freud's theories** of psychoanalysis as **inspiration**.

Late night when sleep eludes my grasp and the air is saturated with a midnight smell of dewy grass, I play Solitaire on my computer. Rarely do I win. Unable to admit failure, I often click on "show me a move" and elect to die a slow death. On a good night, the revealed move will turn over a card that clarifies the board in my mind.

Few nights are good nights.

Jacob and I fought like cats and dogs. He would not, or *could not,* listen to me, and I never took the time to explain. We would squabble and eventually say hurtful things, which we both later regretted. He'd apologize, and I would accept it, pretend I wasn't hurt, and carry on with the series of petty jokes and rivalries that defined our relationship. No matter how right I felt, I claimed to have been in the wrong just to carry on with the general good humor. I continually put my hurt aside and convinced myself I was just being silly.

When I play Solitaire as the midnight alarm blares scathingly from my purple wristwatch, I always promise that if this next card isn't the winning card, I will close the game and retire to my bed. The quilt and pillow are an attractive

For Real?

The concept behind **Halloween** dates back to the 5ᵗʰ century BC in Ireland, even though back then it **wasn't** for kids. When Irish immigrants came to the U.S. in the 1840s, they brought the holiday with them, and eventually trick-or-treating became part of the celebration.

prospect. But it never is just one card, because what if the *next* card is the winner? What if, with just *one more card* . . . ?

On Halloween two years ago, Jacob took a tumble from his pedestal. A group of us were going to a friend's Halloween party dressed as the alter egos we had acquired from a mass reading of *The Lord of the Rings*. Whether or not I wore a plastic sword escapes me, but I do recall comfort, high amusement and a friend commenting that my rain-soaked hair looked like grease, just like my character's. Since Mom had not allowed me to skip showers for three weeks straight, my friend's comment sent my confidence through the roof. This was turning into the best Halloween ever.

Seen It?

The Lord of the Rings trilogy was a magnificant film portrayal of the book series by J. R. R. Tolkien.

Jacob quickly ended that by turning around and snapping at me, "You know, your costume's nothing but brown cloth." He kept talking, but I drowned it out. Hearing him say that hurt. *Why is he being so unkind? We're all having a good time. Why ruin that?*

I stopped talking. Sam, who has always been good to me, fell behind the others so I didn't have to walk alone. He was dressed as the Invisible Man. For that costume I would have given anything, especially when Jacob turned around and

CONSIDER THIS . . .

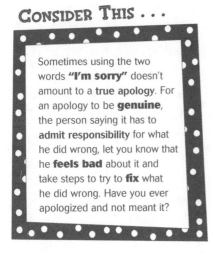

Sometimes using the two words **"I'm sorry"** doesn't amount to a **true apology**. For an apology to be **genuine**, the person saying it has to **admit responsibility** for what he did wrong, let you know that he **feels bad** about it and take steps to try to **fix** what he did wrong. Have you ever apologized and not meant it?

started justifying his earlier comment, conveying my pettiness and his righteousness. I realized then that his apologies had always left me feeling empty because he never actually apologized for anything. He only gave explanations. Not once had I ever heard him say, "I'm sorry."

"Go away," I muttered, more to my feet than to him, but Jacob continued. "Go away!" I repeated again to the road, and again Jacob did not heed.

"Jacob, she really doesn't want to talk to you right now," Sam said. When Jacob snapped at Sam in response, it was all I could do not to kick him.

For the rest of the night, Jacob kept approaching me and trying to defend his comment. I was scrunched in a niche between the party host's desk and her bookcase, and I really just wanted to be left alone. By the end of the night, I wasn't the only one upset—my friend's parents had told Jacob to leave me alone, too.

Since that night, I have hated a boy I once considered to be my closest friend. My most vivid memories of seventh grade involve Jacob and light sabers. But that Halloween, he ruined all of that. When we have been together since, I maintain an air of hostility. After playing the innocent victim for a while, he backs off. Every time, I tell myself it doesn't hurt anymore. And then I think back to my metaphor for Jacob—Solitaire.

Something about the game always drives me to turn over

just one more card. When the sensible side of me kicks in and I finally close down the game and pull the covers up high, I close my eyes and still see the cards. The next night, I click the little blue icon, and a new game is dealt.

Yet to this day, I am unable to deal a new game with Jacob. Any closeness to him results in a churning mass of shame and anger and the fear that I will allow our old unhealthy patterns to reinstate themselves. Sometime in the future, when I am brave, I will brace myself and face my once-friend. When I have the power to separate past from present and tell Jacob that he hurt me without feeling that hurt, I will no longer feel fear or shame.

HOW ABOUT YOU?

Have you ever had a **friend** who **crossed a line** and there was no going back?

That Halloween night, I dressed as a character whose name was Hope. Ironically, that is the one thing I cannot shake—that my relationship with Jacob may one day mend. No matter how hard I try not to, I will always hope.

Deborah Bramwell, age 16

OUTSIDE THE BOX

Do you have a friend who treats you badly? I'm not talking about one or two screw-ups here . . . I mean someone who consistently does things that make you feel not-so-good about yourself? Here is a three-step program for dealing with the problem:

1. Listen to your gut. If interacting with the friend makes you feel like you want to pull your hair out, then most likely there's a serious problem in the dynamic.

2. Get some perspective on the relationship from a parent or older brother or sister to find out if what's going on is typical friendship behavior.

3. Talk to the friend and tell him how you're feeling. A true friend will want to address the issue and keep the friendship on track. If he's not willing to work things out, it's time to move on!

WHEN WE'VE GOT CLOSE FRIENDS, we might make a lot of assumptions about them. We might assume how they feel about us, why they like us . . . even what kind of person they are. So when they do or say something that gives us a hint that they might not be the way we thought, it can be a shock to the system. I remember hanging out with a friend once and she just kind of casually made a racial slur in the cause of normal conversation. I was flabbergasted. Everything I had thought about this friend changed in an instant. She wasn't the person I thought she was. And she wasn't a person I could hang out with anymore.

In this next story, the author discovers her assumptions about her best friend couldn't have been more wrong. And the words that he said so casually one afternoon would change who the author is.

Andy

At twelve years old, I was an awkward-looking girl. My often greasy, dark blonde hair was a shapeless mess, my face was full of angry zits, my fashion sense was nonexistent. My nose was too big for my face, my body was changing from a girl's shape to a woman's, and I was a chubby, funny-looking creature. I never noticed or worried about my appearance. For as long as I could remember, I had been told by adults that I was pretty and not to worry about looks because intelligence was what mattered. With this background, I survived three months of seventh grade in a public school without even one thought about my weight or appearance. I had never learned to be insecure.

Andy was in my home-room. He was beautiful; there was no other way to describe him. Black hair hung over his naturally tan forehead, and his blue eyes sparkled with every look. I would always watch him out of the corner of my eye in class. We became fast friends because we both

loved theatre, singing, dancing and uncontrollable laughter. Soon enough, I was going to his house every day after school until five or six when my mother dragged me home. Not only was Andy my best friend, but I developed the biggest crush on him. I knew that Andy was my first real love, and I had to have him. I was sure that with our continually budding friendship we would be a couple soon enough.

One windy day in April, we were sitting on his roof playing with purple and blue Russian dolls that squeaked unbear-ably when we tried to fit them together. As we fiddled with the decorated wooden toys, Andy started talking about pretty girls in our grade. I listened absently—sometimes we talked about good-looking people in our school, and I always assumed we were flirting—like in movies where the couples try to make each other jealous. "Girls really have to be skinny to be pretty, you know? Well, don't you

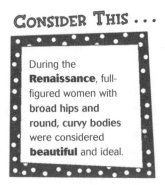

CONSIDER THIS . . .

During the **Renaissance**, full-figured women with **broad hips and round, curvy bodies** were considered **beautiful** and ideal.

know, Liia? Girls really
do have to be skinny."
   I stopped and looked
into his face. He was giving me a meaningful gaze,
like he was trying to tell
me something. "What? I
don't think so . . ." I said.
   "No, really, they do. They
have to be skinny. Girls who are
fat don't ever get boyfriends." He leaned closer
to me. "You should think about that." He flashed a smile,
blushing lightly, and turned to look away.

> ## For Real?
> Wooden Russian nesting dolls
> are called **"matryoshka,"** and
> they're the **classic Russian
> souvenir**. In each set, as
> many as 30 dolls, which are
> identical except for their size,
> are "stacked" inside one another.

   I didn't understand him. I couldn't believe what my
instinct told me, that my best friend, my one true love, my
inevitable middle-school sweetheart, was calling me *fat*. I
knew it couldn't be true, but I had to be sure. "Andy? Do you
think I'm fat?"
   Andy turned to me, his face close enough to kiss. "Well . . .
yeah. You could definitely lose a few pounds. That is, if you
want a boyfriend or . . . like, if you ever want to be pretty.
Then, yeah, you need to lose weight."
   I nodded, for lack of another reaction, and we changed the
subject. When I went home, I left our friendship and my confidence on his bumpy, faded gray rooftop.
   Before my shower that night, I stood in front of the full-
length mirror and critiqued myself. My once beautiful body
was transformed. My hips were too wide . . . too round. My
stomach was fat. *Every* part of me felt fat. My arms jiggled,
my cheeks were too full, my fingers chunky. Andy told me

CONSIDER THIS . . .

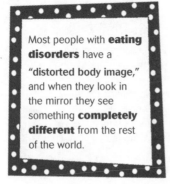

Most people with **eating disorders** have a "distorted body image," and when they look in the mirror they see something **completely different** from the rest of the world.

once that if you could wrap your arms around your waist, one in front and one behind, and have your fingertips touch, then you were the right size. From the first second I thought about trying, I knew my fingertips wouldn't reach. It became my goal to be able to do it.

The next day in school, I avoided Andy. I took different routes, made different friends, sat in different seats. Over the next four months, I went on a strict diet, developing a severe eating disorder. I lost twenty-five pounds and as the sizes dropped, I felt accomplished. In some weird way I was making Andy proud. Midsummer, I wrapped my arms around my waist and my fingertips touched with room to spare.

Andy's comments changed my view of myself forever. I took his one comment and saw flaw after flaw. Although today I'm able to cope with my self-criticism in a healthier way and am eating again, from time to time, I wrap my arms around my waist to make sure I'm still thin enough.

Liia Rudolph, Age 17

OUTSIDE THE BOX

Has someone said something to you that made you question how you feel about yourself? Here are some ways to take back your power and get back to feeling like <u>you</u>:

- Challenge what the person said and consider what their motivation was in saying it.
- Ask yourself these questions: Who made them the expert, anyway? Why am I giving them so much power?
- Look to other friends and family to give you perspective.

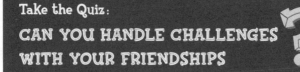

Take the Quiz:

CAN YOU HANDLE CHALLENGES WITH YOUR FRIENDSHIPS

1. You've been dying to hang out with the charismatic new girl in school. She seems to have it all—good looks, good fashion, good sense of humor. Even a smile from her makes you feel like a million bucks. But when you finally get into her inner circle, you find she's got a mean streak and likes to pick on another group of girls. You . . .

   ___ A. let it slide. You're so happy that she thinks you're important enough to hang out with that you can't bear to rock the boat. You don't have to participate in the tormenting if you don't want to.

   ___ B. try to overlook her bad behavior, hoping it was just a misunderstanding. When you realize it's the real deal, you decide not to hang out with her when she's picking on the girls. Any other time, it's okay.

   ___ C. are shocked by her bad form and get out of that friendship really fast. There's no use developing a strong friendship when the two of you couldn't be more different.

2. A nasty rumor about your BFF starts circulating around the school. The rumor is so out of control that you can foresee your rep going down right along with your friend's if nothing is done. How do you handle it? You . . .

   ___ A. try to stay out of it and not get in the middle, thinking, *What if the rumors are true after all?* You don't want to risk the reputation you've worked so hard to build.

   ___ B. confront your friend and ask her if the rumors are true, and only when she completely denies them do you support her 100 percent.

___ C. stand up and defend your friend anytime you have a chance and do your best to put a stop to it. If you can't get anywhere, you take it to the school guidance counselor and deal with the problem.

3. You are selected to be part of a countywide after-school program for gifted students, but you are panicking because no one from your group of friends is going to take part. You'd rather not, especially considering how shy you can be with strangers, but your parents aren't giving you any choice in the matter. What do you do? You . . .

___ A. skip out on the program the first week, telling your parents you missed the bus and had no way to get there. You spend the next week begging and pleading with your parents to let you drop out of the program.

___ B. agree to go, but don't make any effort to become friends with anyone. If you keep to yourself and mind your own business, hopefully you'll survive this after-school nightmare.

___ C. stay up the night before the first day and plan out a strategy for handling what might be an uncomfortable situation. After all, you've got a great group of friends at school, so they obviously saw something in you they liked. Hopefully, these kids will, too.

4. You're in your room surfing the Web one afternoon when you get an e-mail from someone in school saying some pretty terrible stuff about another girl in your school. You click on a link and are even more horrified to find that there is a blog online dedicated to making this girl look terrible. You . . .

___ A. are shocked about it, but forward the e-mail to a few friends. You know they'd want to see it, whether it's true stuff or not.

___ B. shake your head with disgust and delete the e-mail. There's nothing else you can do.

___ C. write back to the person who sent the e-mail to you and nicely ask them to stop sending you this kind of stuff. Then you show the e-mail to your mom or dad or teacher to make them aware of the cyber bullying.

5. You and your friend have been slowly befriending a group of cool girls. You're hopeful about being made official members of their clique. But when the head of the clique tells you that you're welcome to join while your friend's not, you're at a loss. How do you handle it? You . . .

    ___ A. decide to join anyway and try to maintain a separate friendship with your BFF. She doesn't have to be involved in everything you do, does she?

    ___ B. ask your BFF what she thinks you should do. If she isn't too upset, then you can join and not feel bad about it.

    ___ C. politely say, "Thanks, but no thanks," and decline joining. If your BFF isn't good enough to hang out with them, then you're not interested.

Well, what do you think? Give yourself 10 points for every A, 20 points for every B and 30 points for every C. Look below to find out how ready you are to handle some friendship challenges:

50–70 points = Yikes! It looks like you need a little more experience handling tough spots in friendships. The next time a tough situation comes up, take a minute to step back and think about it from a different perspective before you react.

80–120 points = You're ready to handle some challenges, but you don't see everything as black and white. As you go through more experiences with your friendships, you'll probably be a little more assured in your responses.

130–150 points = Wow! Where'd you learn all this stuff? You're ready for whatever challenges to your friendships come along.

CHAPTER 3

FRIENDS WHO INSPIRE

Every now and then, a friend comes along who inspires us . . . to be a better person, to dream big, to be ourselves. Sometimes these friends aren't even aware of the power they have to affect us this way—they do it just by being who they are. This chapter is about these inspirational friendships and looks at how we can be inspirational to those around us, too.

I HAVE THIS ONE FRIEND WHOM I SEE ONLY ABOUT ONCE A YEAR, and during the in-between months, we talk maybe once or twice on the phone. But whenever I visit her hometown, I always carve out a big chunk of time for her because I know that once we get together, you'll have to pry us apart. Hours will fly by as we share stories, laugh and relate to each other in a way that I don't with too many other people.

For Real?

Worn and **faded Levi's** are a **hot-ticket** item these days. A single pair of vintage Levi's can fetch more than **$300**, depending on their condition!

There is something to be said for friendships that are so strong, so comfy, that, like a pair of old jeans, it still feels right no matter how long since you've been together. And like an old pair of jeans, these friends know your every faded edge, your every ripped seam . . . every last worn hole. Why do some friendships stay connected with little effort, and when you're reunited you can pick up right where you left off the last time?

When I have these sorts of connections, I always wonder if maybe the friend and I were sisters in a past life or something. What else would account for that feeling of instant comfort? I can't explain it, but I can say that when these friends come along, they're worth holding on to.

CONSIDER THIS . . .

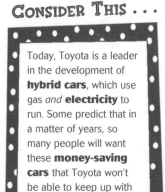

Today, Toyota is a leader in the development of **hybrid cars**, which use gas *and* **electricity** to run. Some predict that in a matter of years, so many people will want these **money-saving cars** that Toyota won't be able to keep up with the demand.

Take Care

"Take care!" I yelled.

I stood beneath the garage door, leaning against my father's Toyota, watching the teal minivan crawl slowly out of our driveway.

My mom stood next to me, fiercely waving and profusely crying. My father was on her right, and as he watched, his keen blue eyes suddenly looked aged and worn. Together we stared with longing at the small hands pressed against the van's windows and the man in the driver's seat mouthing "good-bye."

"There they go again . . ."

* * *

This was no once-in-a-lifetime event. It wasn't a movie or TV show where the episode ends and life resumes normality. This scene happens two or three times a year, and it's far too real for my taste. Every December, I stand barefoot on the smooth, cold cement, my hair frumpy and tangled from an evening spent wrestling on sleeping bags, and watch with teary eyes as that green van departs for its very own garage in Canyon Lake, Texas.

Those hands pressed against the windows belong to my best friends, Jamie and Jerry. It would be another six months before I would see them again, hence my misery.

Seen It?

Saying good-bye to those we love can be hard, no doubt. Have you ever seen the classic good-bye scenes in any of these movies?

- *Casablanca* (1942), when Rick (Humphrey Bogart) says good-bye to Ilsa (Ingrid Bergman) at the airport.
- *Wizard of Oz* (1939), when Dorothy says good-bye to the Scarecrow, Tin Man and Lion before clicking her ruby red slippers and saying, "There's no place like home."
- *Dirty Dancing* (1987), when Baby (Jennifer Grey) bids Johnny (Patrick Swayze) *adios* before he tears his car down a dirt road.

I know I should be used to it by now. Their family hasn't lived near mine for as long as I can remember. They've moved to San Antonio, Burleson and then Canyon Lake—all more than three hours away from my small hometown of San Angelo. But if there's one thing I've learned, it's that distance is relative. Your friends are never farther from you than you want them to be. True friendship is something no amount of distance can break.

* * *

"Oh, my gosh!" Jamie exclaimed, her face turning red as she laughed.

"Ha ha! I can't believe you just called the White House!"

"Dude, we should call back and ask if we can talk to Georgie Boy," Jerry said.

It was the summer of 2004. I sat

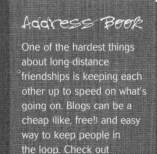

Address Book

One of the hardest things about long-distance friendships is keeping each other up to speed on what's going on. Blogs can be a cheap (like, free!) and easy way to keep people in the loop. Check out *www.blogger.com* for more information.

on Jerry's bottom bunk bed, staring at a phone number listed in a novel. We had just dialed it on a cell phone, and we were shocked to discover the phone number wasn't only legitimate . . . it was a line to the White House Secretary.

CONSIDER THIS . . .

Ever notice that when characters in TV shows or the movies dial a phone number, it always begins with the three numbers 555? **555 doesn't exist** as a real telephone exchange, so there can be no chance of broadcasing a real person's phone number by accident.

"Are you absolutely positive that that lady wasn't teasing you?" I asked.

"Of course! She said 'White House Secretary speaking,'" Jamie replied, looking almost too innocent for a girl of thirteen. Jerry and I, the older and wiser of our trio (fifteen and sixteen), had little time to question her motives before their mom, Cheryl, stormed in.

"You called *where?*"

Whoops.

"Well, Mom, it might have just been some lady playing a joke," Jerry said, slowly talking his way out of it even though we had looked up the area code online, and it was definitely in the District of Columbia.

My mom dragged me into the bathroom and gave me the usual speech about being a responsible young lady. I ignored her and soon returned to a more stimulating conversation with my friends about government cover-ups, aliens and souls of the undead.

When I'm with Jamie and Jerry, my sanity flies right out the window, and I'm no longer on the verge of becoming an adult. I'm simply a kid enjoying myself and letting loose with my best friends. There's no feeling in the world more comforting than that. I could be a brilliant genius or a mindless fool—Jamie and Jerry would love me just the same.

"Take care!" they yelled as we drove away.

Jerry and Jamie and their family stood waving until we were out of sight.

HOW ABOUT YOU?

Do you have any **long-distance friendships?** What is your **secret** to making them work?

When we left that day, Mom was crying again, and so was I. My parents didn't want to leave their friends any more than I wanted to leave mine, but we had to. The only thing that got us through was the knowledge that they'd be visiting us in December.

* * *

"Well, what do you believe, then?" Jerry asked.

"I don't know," I replied, frustrated. "I'm just not much of a religious person. I don't know what I believe yet. I just don't want people pressuring me all the time to join their churches."

"I'm not trying to pressure you. I just don't think it's good to be without faith," Jerry said, whispering to me over Jamie's sleeping bag.

"But there's so many religions, and they all say basically the same thing . . ." I replied.

"Yeah, but that's the beauty of it. Take Buddhism and Christianity . . . they're just slightly different paths to get the same results," he said, cutting me off, but making his point.

We sat in silence for a few moments after that, glancing at the clock. 4:30 AM.

He settled back into his sleeping bag. "Oh . . . I've figured out what I want to be," Jerry said casually.

Read It?

In Judy Blume's classic *Are You There, God? It's Me, Margaret,* Margaret explores **different religions** to see what **feels** right for her.

"Really?" I asked with a sarcastic smile. "Let me guess . . . a psychiatrist? A ghostbuster?"

"A director," he replied.

I settled back and listened. He told me how much he respected directors and loved movies, how he could just enter that fantasy world and stay there sometimes. At first I took his words with a grain of salt. His big ideas about things like that were always short-lived.

"I think I'd make a good director. I've got some ideas for plots, and I love characters," he went on. "And you know me and my artistic side."

Indeed, I did.

"That's going to take work," I said, trying not to sound condescending. "Dreams like that don't come true for everyone, you know."

"I could do it," he said.

WHERE DO YOU STAND?

Do your friends inspire you to dream big or to be a better person? Find out below:

My BFF listens to me ramble on about my career goals.

A. ALWAYS   B. NOT USUALLY

I feel safe to share everything with my circle of friends.

A. ALWAYS   B. NOT USUALLY

My friends are always there to support me when I'm challenging myself in a sport or other activity.

A. ALWAYS   B. NOT USUALLY

My BFF doesn't compete with me even though we're both pursuing the same goals.

A. ALWAYS   B. NOT USUALLY

Watching my friend pursue his or her goals inspires me to do the same with mine.

A. ALWAYS   B. NOT USUALLY

How'd ya do?
Mostly As = You've got great friends who'll help you go far.
Mostly Bs = Your friends may be holding you back from reaching your potential. Try supporting them more, and maybe they'll respond by doing the same.

CONSIDER THIS . . .

It's never too early to **start dreaming big** about the **future.** In fact, **teens** with clear goals about the future are much more likely to see their dreams realized when they get older, mostly because they've figured out what they want and are **focused** on **making it happen**.

It took me a few minutes to digest what he meant by that. The look on his face lingered. Even in the dark, I could see his blue eyes shining.

That's the beauty of our friendship. When we're together, we let our craziest fears and ideas out in the open. There's nothing like sharing problems, solutions and that sense of confidence and relief when everyone feels the same way.

"Take care!"

Chelsea Preas, age 17

DO YOU EVER NOTICE THAT THERE ARE FRIENDSHIPS that require lots of work and others that are as natural as peanut butter and jelly? There are friendships that offer simple companionship and others that offer a shoulder to cry on. Some friends might lend you a hat, while others would take the shirts off their backs to give it to you. As this next poem explores, some friendships just work effortlessly. When they do, it's a great thing.

For Real?

While it's not known when **PB&J sandwiches** were first invented, they became popular in the U.S. during WWII, when protein sources like meat were really expensive. PB&J was a cheap, relatively nutritious meal.

OUTSIDE THE BOX

Has it been months since you've seen a close friend? Sometimes when you get together after a long time apart, it's like you've never been away from each other. But other times, it may feel a little awkward. Here are some ideas for rekindling the friendship in a jiffy:

- Flip through a photo album full of pics from your past together . . . you'll be reminiscing in no time.
- Do something or go somewhere that has special significance for the two of you.
- Put on some music that reminds you of the time when the two of you weren't so far apart.
- Be honest about how you're feeling and talk it through with your friend. Then you can work together to get things back where they were, or maybe even take your relationship to a whole new level!

True Friends

When you feel all alone
Like there's nothing left
No one to turn to
People turn their backs
No one listens
No one cares
And when you need someone
   most
No one is there

HOW ABOUT YOU?

Have you ever had a friend **step up** and **be there** for you when you **needed** her most?

You failed at life
You aren't worth a darn
Tried to do the best you can
Cry out, but no one hears
No one is there to wipe your tears

The world it weighs
You down and so
You fall deeper in a hole
You thought your life was great and
   then
Took a turn for the worst
Won't start again

CONSIDER THIS . . .

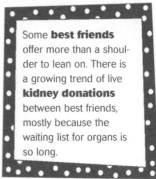

Some **best friends** offer more than a shoulder to lean on. There is a growing trend of live **kidney donations** between best friends, mostly because the waiting list for organs is so long.

That's when you have to open your eyes
Then you will start to realize
That you aren't alone after all
Someone is catching you as you fall
A friend listens to the burdens you bear

Showing you that they really do care
You are worth everything to them
They know you do the best you can
When you cry so much it makes a river of tears
They make it so a bridge appears

When the world weighs you down
They are there to help
When you fall in a hole
They dig you out
You were lost and so they found
A way to turn your life around
And they don't do it because they can
They do it because they are your friend

C.C. Frick, age 16

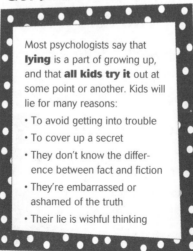

CONSIDER THIS . . .

Most psychologists say that **lying** is a part of growing up, and that **all kids try it** out at some point or another. Kids will lie for many reasons:

- To avoid getting into trouble
- To cover up a secret
- They don't know the difference between fact and fiction
- They're embarrassed or ashamed of the truth
- Their lie is wishful thinking

WHEN I WAS FIFTEEN, I would have laughed at the suggestion that perhaps my parents were actually my best friends. My *parents*? You mean the ones who had the magical ability to tell if I was lying even when I came up with a real doozy? Or the ones who were so overprotective of me that I couldn't ride my bike past the big rock at the end of the street? Or the ones who called my friend's parents to make sure they'd be home during a weekend sleepover?

Friends? On the contrary, many times I thought of my parents as enemies. The ones who were always trying to squash my good time and ensure that I didn't have too much fun, get too crazy or enjoy too much freedom.

But what if freedom from my parents was all I had, and I was stuck in the foster-care system like the author of this next poem? *My Two Best Friends* makes you stop and think about the things many of us take for granted. Who would have thought that as a teenager, our parental units could be our closest friends?

My Two Best Friends

Nine schools and nine cities in fifteen years.
Making friends pretty pointless.
Foster kids easily learn how not to feel.

Then they came and expected me to
    be happy.
Promises given so often to my
    younger sister, Dani, and I.
Promises that quickly became lies.
Why should they be different?

Seen It?

The movie *White Oleander* (2002) is a haunting tale of a teenage girl, Astrid, immersed in the **foster-care** system.

So I didn't come willingly.
I almost had to be dragged out of
    the last home.
My hands touched none of my
    suitcases.
I would go to the new school,
But liking it was another question.

Read It?

The novel *Ellen Foster* by
Kaye Gibbons is about a
young **orphan** who is
shuttled from home to home.

Her, I especially wanted to hate.
She wanted to cook for me, talk to me, even tuck me in . . .
All the things a "mother" would do.
Her warm words were quickly silenced by my cold ones.

He, the one who loved her so.
He was always quiet,
Surprisingly, never raising a hand.
Not even when Dani wet the bed purposefully
And threw the glass plate on the floor.

The breaking point—
The hand I raised and the words I said;
Even HBO would frown.
They both looked at me without speaking.

Finally, she said,
"We loved you before we ever saw you.
We had a choice, and you were it. Get it all out because
    we're never letting you go.
When you get married, you still have to live here. Kids and all."

And I couldn't help but smile.
They were and continue to be a year later

Still ridiculously goofy.
But I've taught them about music
   and fashion,
And they, my mom and dad, my two
   best friends,
Have taught my sister and me about
   love.

Jalesa Harper, age 15

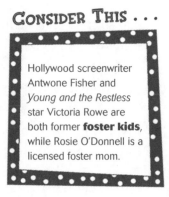

CONSIDER THIS . . .

Hollywood screenwriter Antwone Fisher and *Young and the Restless* star Victoria Rowe are both former **foster kids**, while Rosie O'Donnell is a licensed foster mom.

Spotlight On ... FOSTER CARE

What is foster care, anyway? Foster care is a system that's set up so that kids who are abused, neglected or abandoned can be placed in a temporary home with adult caregivers. While adopted children's parents become the child's legal guardian, foster kids are a state's responsibility. Sometimes, foster parents decide to adopt their foster kids, and then they can become full members of the family. There are more than 500,000 kids in the foster-care system today.

As you can probably guess, being a foster kid places a lot more stress on teens than those who live with their parents. Here are just a few statistics to show you how hard it is for these kids:

- Only half of all foster kids graduate from high school.
- Up to 40 percent of former foster kids end up on welfare or in jail.
- Former foster kids are four times as likely to be homeless.

For kids in the foster-care system with brothers and sisters, the situation is even more difficult because many families are only interested in housing one child and often the siblings are separated.

May is National Foster Care month. For more information on foster care, check out *www.fostercaremonth .org/Home.*

I WAS A FRESHMAN. SHE WAS A SENIOR. And boy, could she run! My first mentor, Sue, was a 400-meter-dash runner who kicked some serious butt every time she got on the track. And for some reason, she took a special interest in me, this pipsqueak of a kid with a loud mouth and a goofy sense of humor.

In many ways, Sue became the big sister I never had. Wait a minute . . . I *did* have a big sister. Well, let's just say that Sue treated me like the little sister *she* never had. She'd laugh at my jokes, let me hang out with her on the benches between classes and cheer me on during track workouts, encouraging me to run harder and push myself.

To have this person whom I admired so much believe in me was incredible. I felt so special to have her looking out for me, like her approval meant that I was somebody special myself.

Sue was the first, but I've been lucky enough to have many mentors along the way. And whenever I have the chance, I try to give it back by paying it forward.

HOW ABOUT YOU?

Has an **older student** ever taken you **under** his or her **wing**? How did it feel?

THE WORD

A **mentor** is another word for a teacher or counselor—**someone you can trust**.

A Different Kind of Friend

I never thought that one of my very best friends would be twelve years older than me. But it's true. I, the girl who used to laugh at the idea, have a mentor. Two years ago, when I was a sophomore in high school, my former youth leader, Judy, came up to me in church.

"Hey, Sarah," she said, "I've been praying about this, and I'd really like to start meeting with you weekly—doing a Bible study, talking, just getting to know each other on a deeper level."

I was touched beyond words. This tall, slim, beautiful woman the

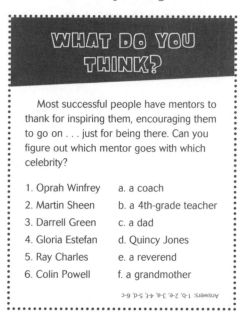

WHAT DO YOU THINK?

Most successful people have mentors to thank for inspiring them, encouraging them to go on . . . just for being there. Can you figure out which mentor goes with which celebrity?

1. Oprah Winfrey   a. a coach
2. Martin Sheen   b. a 4th-grade teacher
3. Darrell Green   c. a dad
4. Gloria Estefan   d. Quincy Jones
5. Ray Charles   e. a reverend
6. Colin Powell   f. a grandmother

Answers: 1-b, 2-e, 3-a, 4-f, 5-d, 6-c

girls in my youth group wanted to emulate had just asked *me* if I wanted to hang out with her! "Wow—I'd love that!"

"Great! Are you free for dinner sometime this week?"

And so it began.

Judy surprised me with her realness. Whenever we met, she didn't compel me to spill all my problems. Instead, she waited until I felt like sharing whatever was on my heart, and when I did (it didn't take long), she never once made me feel like a patient she was counseling. She came down to my level and showed me how she solved similar problems in her life

For Real?

According to Big Brothers/
Big Sisters, students who have a
mentor are **46% less likely**
to start taking illegal **drugs**,
27% less likely to try **drinking**
alcohol and **52% less likely**
to **skip** out on school.

when she was my age. She does that to this day. She listens to me . . . *really* listens. She supports me, no matter what.

During my junior year, I went through a difficult situation and, surprisingly, when I talked to Judy about it, begging her to understand my point of view, she didn't give me the whole, "Well, this is what you could have done differently" speech. She took my side and let me know that I was doing just fine with how I handled it. I needed to hear that she supported me. I needed to hear that an adult understood that sometimes a teenager is right.

Judy also treats me like an equal. I spent the night at her house once, and we lounged around in our PJs watching reality shows and talking about deep issues. And not just my personal issues . . . hers, too. She doesn't mind talking with me about her struggles, and because of that, I feel like I can share mine.

Judy is one of my most precious sources of encouragement. I constantly receive sweet notes that simply say, "I hope you're having a good week! You mean so much to me!" She encourages me in other ways, too. Once the question, "Who is a person you look up to and admire in your life?" came up in our Bible study book. She wrote my name in the blank and listed several character qualities she admires about me. That encouragement went straight to my heart and stayed there.

Address Book

Are you looking for a mentor to help guide you in your school, college and career dreams? For more information and a list of mentoring organizations by state, check out www.mentoring.org

I left my high school when I was a junior, and the change tore me up inside. For a while, I thought I was depressed, and even when I told her that, she let me know that I had made a good decision to leave and that life would only get better (she was right—it did), and that she was behind me the whole way. Judy's got it all—she's real, she's supportive, she's encouraging, and she treats me equally. But the quality I love most about her is that she genuinely loves me. It's not often you meet a person who knows all your flaws and still seems only to notice the good. That's what I've found in Judy. I have few of what I would call "best friends," and she is undoubtedly one of them.

Beth Marshall, age 17

OUTSIDE THE BOX

Are you in a tough situation with your friends, family or school? Here are four ideas for handling the emotional ride you're on:

- Write about it . . . spill your thoughts out of your head and onto paper.
- Go on a date with yourself to give yourself a break from the situation. Go to a goofy movie, an art exhibit, the mall . . .
- Spend five minutes every day meditating by sitting quietly with your eyes closed and focusing on breathing deeply.
- Come up with an affirmation and repeat it to yourself every time you start to get upset about the situation. An example of a good affirmation is: <u>I can choose to be happy no matter what the circumstance.</u>

Spotlight On ... MENTORS

Ask any successful adults how they got where they are, and chances are they'll mention the impact of a mentor in their lives. Mentors can come in all shapes, sizes and ages—from an older sibling to a teacher to a camp counselor. You might have even sought out a mentor to support you in reaching one of your goals.

Relationships with mentors can last a lifetime. These powerful influences add so much to your life, such as . . .

- giving advice about how to handle difficult situations
- offering job advice and career guidance
- providing a reference for a college or job application
- playing the role of a big brother or sister
- offering a different perspective.

Mentors don't have to live in the same town as you do. In fact, many people communicate with mentors over the phone or via e-mail or IM. The most important thing is finding a mentor who understands your goals and can be a support in helping you reach them. You don't have to be limited to one mentor, either. You could have one mentor for your future college and career goals and another one to support you on your quest to be the best soccer player around. Whatever works for you.

For Real?

You might know that **Ashlee Simpson** is a successful singer and actress, but did you also know that at the age of eleven, she was the **youngest person** ever to be admitted into the **School of American Ballet**?

DO ME A FAVOR. Grab a photo album or turn on your computer and check out all your digital pics. Now find a picture of you and a friend, or maybe a whole group of you, where you look happy. Focus on the picture. How do you feel? Can you remember the emotions you were feeling at the moment the picture was taken? Were you genuinely happy? Laughing? Hysterical? Were you doing something special or just hanging out in the backyard? Was it taken on an "everyday" or a special occasion?

Now put the picture away and close your eyes. Can you still conjure up those same feelings? Can you remember a time when you and your friends were hanging out, having a ball, and you felt one hundred percent content? This next story is a great reminder to stop and smell the roses of friendship.

The Gift of Friendship

The music blares, and Ashlee Simpson can be heard faintly over my four girlfriends and my singing along. The windows are all rolled down, sweeping that summer smell through the car and sending our slightly out of tune but proud voices onto the streets. We are five seniors-to-be, packed into my small Honda Civic, driving the winding river road for the last time this summer. We are going to our paradise—the

THE WORD

Having an **epiphany** means to **suddenly realize** the significance of something.

lake. Each curve sends our bare, browned knees bumping together as we sit cramped but completely comfortable. I stop singing for a moment and look at the girls around me. Not noticing that I have stopped singing, each of them continues on without a thought, but my brain starts buzzing, and I have an epiphany. As I think about each of the girls, I realize how lucky I am to be blessed with the great gift of friendship. It is so often overlooked, but at moments like this, you catch a glimpse of the importance friendship truly holds.

I know these girls, and they know me. I remember all we have been through together, all the joy and, yes, at times, the pain. Each memory is tucked safely somewhere in my brain, but, more important, deep in my heart. Like the time the girls and I stayed up all night reading on the roof to finish a book that was due the next day. As the sun came up around the neighborhood, each of us put our books down and took a moment to watch the breathtaking sunrise. Or the day when a friend of thirteen years had to move away. We all cried together, but we knew that the move wouldn't change a thing between us. Now, five years later, she is singing along with us as if we never had missed a day.

HOW ABOUT YOU?

When you're having a great day, do you ever **step back** and realize how **happy** you are at that very **moment**?

CONSIDER THIS . . .

> Do you know the saying, **"Wake up and smell the coffee"**? Well, that's just another way of saying, **"Live in the moment!"** When we take the time to **appreciate everyday** moments and times when we're truly happy, it helps us get through the more difficult times.

It is at times like this that I can't help but wonder what I would be like without the influence of these girls. Would I be who and where I am today if I didn't have those girls to lean on, to learn from or to trust through my life? I can't imagine what it is like for those who walk throughout life without the love and companionship of close friendships.

Now, every time I pass that winding river road, I catch myself reminiscing about all the good times I have shared with my friends. I love that I have those friendships to think about, to warm my heart and to put a smile on my face. And I love that I will always have the gift of friendship to cherish.

Jennifer Traylor, age 18

Seen It?

In *Boys in the Side* (1994), Whoopie Goldberg, Mary Louise Parker and Drew Barrymore form a great friendship during a road trip across the country.

Take the Quiz:
DO YOU KNOW HOW TO BE AN INSPIRATIONAL FRIEND

1. Your BFF has been down and unmotivated lately. He isn't making his grades, didn't make the cut for varsity and is starting to feel like it's a waste of time to keep working hard in school. Which of the following is closer to what you'd do?

____ A. It's really a drag when he gets like this, so you opt to get some distance so you don't get sucked down in depression with him.

____ B. You want to help him but aren't sure what to do. You decide to try to distract him by doing things you used to do with him. At the very least, you hope to get his mind off of things.

____ C. You've seen your friend go down this path before and want to inspire him to realize that he can improve in all these areas if he tries. You decide to show him by example, and invite him over to study and work on drills.

2. Auditions are coming up for the class play, and you and your friend are planning to try out. The night before auditions, your friend is a bundle of nerves and calls you late-night for some help. How do you handle it?

____ A. You're slightly annoyed that your friend has trouble handling this kind of stuff. After all, it's late and you have to get sleep, too, so you don't show up at the audition with circles under your eyes. You briefly talk to your friend, suggest she watch TV to distract herself and get off the phone.

____ B. You want to be supportive of your friend, but also think that she needs to learn how to deal with her anxiety. You try to give her a little pep talk on the phone, and then say goodnight.

___ C. It's hard watching your friend get so worked up over an audition. You've never had a problem with nerves before, but you can sympathize. You make arrangements to meet your friend before school to go over the audition material, so she will know it like the back of her hand.

3. It's time to pick classes for the next semester, and your friend wants your advice about what electives to take. He's really interested in marine biology, but he's afraid that his dream career is way out of his league, especially when his family rolls their eyes every time he mentions it. How do you help him?

___ A. You're not sure why he's so worried about his course load, especially since you picked your own schedule, no problem. You didn't have anyone to help you figure it out, so why should your friend be any different?

___ B. You don't want to discourage him, but you've heard that the AP biology class he needs to take is pretty tough, and you're just not sure he can handle it, so you try and convince him to take a general course now and keep his options open.

___ C. You believe that anything is attainable with the right effort and motivation, so you share your own career dreams of going to Harvard and being a lawyer. You let him know that "can't" isn't a part of your vocabulary and doesn't have to be part of his.

4. The state soccer championships are tonight, and your BFF is the star goalie. You know that college recruiters will be at the game and so does your friend, who is anxious about whether or not she'll have what it takes to get a scholarship. What do you do?

___ A. You're really not up for going to the game, and you figure your friend will be too busy playing to realize you're not there anyway. You'll call her up later and see how it went.

___ B. You go to the game and end up watching only half of it because you're hanging out with your other friends. You're there to support your BFF and feel that your presence is support enough.

_____ C. You believe in your friend and want to make sure she goes into the game feeling as empowered as ever, so you make her a CD with a ton of inspirational songs on it to get her fired up.

5. One of your friends has been overweight as long as you can remember, and she's suddenly starting to look thinner. You know she's been exercising and eating better, and you see it's paying off. What would you do?

_____ A. Secretly, you're a little jealous at the great shape your friend is getting into, so you don't say anything. Besides, she might start to think that she's "all that" if she gets too many compliments.

_____ B. You're not sure if it's cool to say anything about her new figure, because then it would be like saying she was fat before. You decide to keep your impressions to yourself.

_____ C. You are so proud of your friend for the hard work she's putting in and want to make sure she knows it, so you buy her a card and slip it into her locker, telling her how great she looks and congratulating her for sticking with her new fitness regime.

So, are you an inspirational friend? Give yourself 10 points for every A, 20 points for every B and 30 points for every C. How'd you do?

50–70 points = It seems as though you've got the power to inspire and support others, but you just haven't realized it yet. Just as a little support can go a long way, the lack of it can have an impact, too. Try to pay more attention to what's going on in your friends' lives, and realize that every little thing you do (or don't do) can have a huge impact.

80–120 points = Believe it or not, you have the power to have a great positive influence on the people around you—you just haven't realized it yet. People are inspired by others who are self-assured, thoughtful, know how to listen to a friend and know when it's time to speak up. Give it a try, and you might find your friends are responding to you differently.

130–150 points = Nice work! There's no doubt that you're an inspiration to everyone who comes in contact with you. You know that the best way to inspire others is to set a good example. If you're positive, dedicated and inspired yourself, people will want to follow your lead. Just by being yourself, you inspire others to be the best they can be.

CHAPTER 4

UNUSUAL FRIENDSHIPS

There's no aisle in the supermarket for friends, and you can't find them on eBay (or maybe you can?). Usually, they show up where we least expect them. And when they do, they aren't always what we expected when we set out to make friends. This chapter looks at how friendships come in all shapes and sizes . . . even species.

> WHILE I WOULDN'T *EVER* WANT TO BE A PRESCHOOLER AGAIN, there is something really great about that age. Everything is a new experience. Life is just one big game of "let's explore," and like sponges, children soak it all in, in their quest to make sense of their world.
>
> I think one of the coolest things about preschoolers is that they're nonjudgmental. If a preschooler sees someone in a wheelchair for the first time, his first instinct isn't that there's something *wrong* with that person . . . it's just that the person is *different* from him. To a preschooler, being different isn't a bad thing . . . it's just, well, *different.*

A Friendship Never Broken

Get out!"

Those were the first words I exchanged with Laura when I was only five years old. She had walked in on me when I was using the bathroom in our kindergarten room. I was so mad. I remember going home and telling my mom all about this "bad" girl who opened the door on me. Little did I know that by opening that bathroom door, Laura would step into my life and open many other doors for me. She would change my life forever.

For Real?

About **1 in every 800** babies will suffer from **Down's syndrome**, which is a genetic condition that results in mental and developmental delays.

Laura has Down's syndrome and was being mainstreamed at my school. After the bathroom incident, my mother sat me down and explained that Laura was "special." She tried to get my five-year-old mind to understand about Laura's mental retardation. I went to

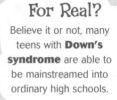

For Real?

Believe it or not, many teens with **Down's syndrome** are able to be mainstreamed into ordinary high schools.

school the next day and decided to try to become Laura's friend. It wasn't very hard. Laura was playful, adventurous and full of giggles. She followed me everywhere, and I doted on her constantly. A few weeks into the school year, we declared each other "best friends."

Seen It?

The sitcom *Life Goes On,* which ran on ABC for four years in the early 1990s, starred Chris Burke, an **actor** with **Down's syndrome.** Burke is still acting, most recently playing a small role in *Mona Lisa Smile* (2003).

For the next two years, Laura and I were put into the same classroom. My other friends got to know her better, and every year she sat next to me at my birthday party. We went to each other's houses to play, hung out at the park together, and she even got her ears pierced like I

did. Laura counted on me to take care of her more and more with each passing year. By the time second grade rolled around, the principal decided that Laura needed to be in a different class from me. She wanted Laura to expand her capabilities and rely less on me. We were upset about it, but we still remained "best friends."

Laura sparked an interest deep inside of me that I don't think I would have discovered without her friendship. I

CONSIDER THIS . . .

A lot of schools today offer **Life Skills** classes. These classes typically **teach** teens about **practical things in life**: finding and keeping a job, how to make the transition from home to independent living, dealing with challenges and making decisions.

became very passionate about disabled kids. I spent a lot of recesses in the Physical Support Room at our school, playing with kids who were in wheelchairs or who couldn't communicate with words. I loved the feeling I got when these kids smiled at me because I came to see them. I volunteered at a Cerebral Palsy Center when I was seven years old. Every other Saturday, I would go there and interact with disabled children— singing songs or playing games. Spending time with these kids made me consider becoming a special-education teacher.

When we were in fourth grade, Laura switched schools and was placed in a Life Skills class. I didn't see her every day, but a few months later, she moved into my neighborhood. Now I could walk to her house and see her whenever I wanted. This made us both feel better about her being at a different school.

As I have gotten older, I have become busier with soccer, field hockey and other friends. Laura and I don't see each other as often as we used to, but we are back in the same school. We are thirteen now and in middle school. She is still in a Life Skills class, and once a week I spend my lunch period volunteering in her classroom. And when it's time for me to leave, Laura always yells out, "I'll call you tonight, Nikki." She wants her classmates to hear this because she is so proud to be my friend, just like I'm proud to be hers.

Laura has taught me a lot, and by showing my peers that it's okay to have a friend with Down's, I hope that I am showing others about being accepting and open to kids with disabilities. Laura has been like any other friend of mine. Sometimes she makes me laugh; sometimes she makes me cry. Sometimes she even embarrasses me. But these are all things that my other friends do, too. Laura is really not that different from everyone else. She loves to try on clothes, watch movies and always talks about her latest boyfriend. And while my mind will continue to grow, Laura's will stop where it is. But that's okay, because our friendship keeps on growing. And so does my perspective of children with disabilities.

Nikki Kremer, age 13

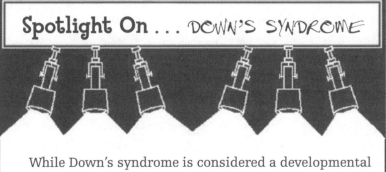

Spotlight On ... DOWN'S SYNDROME

While Down's syndrome is considered a developmental disability, no two teens with Down's syndrome are alike. Here are some facts about Down's syndrome:

- Some children experience difficulty with hearing when younger.
- Learning abilities vary—some have only minor problems learning and reading, and others find it much more difficult.

- Half of all Down's syndrome babies are born with congenital heart defects.
- Many Down's children need to wear glasses to correct vision problems.
- Many children with Down's syndrome grow up to lead normal adult lives and are able to go to college, work, support themselves and live independently—even fall in love and get married!

Because people used to assume kids with Down's syndrome would never be able to read and write, it's only been in the past thirty years that children with Down's syndrome have been going to school. Even then, they were sent to special schools for children with disabilities. It's only been in the past few years that Down's syndrome children have been going to regular schools with everyone else. And guess what? It's been working! Down's syndrome students benefit greatly from being a part of a normal school setting, and their language and social skills have skyrocketed as a result.

For more information about Down's syndrome, check out the National Down Syndrome Society at *www.ndss.org*.

CONSIDER THIS . . .

Some studies have found that a lot of **twins** seem to **know** what the other is thinking and can even **feel** each other's physical pain!

I'VE ALWAYS ENVIED IDENTICAL TWINS. Not necessarily because of the whole matching clothes thing or the endless possibilities for messing with people. No, I envied twins for the incredible bond . . . the whole built-in-best-friend-thing most of them seem to have going on.

I've never known a set of twins, fraternal or identical, same sex or not, who weren't so close that even a crowbar couldn't tear them apart. That kind of unconditional loyalty and love just seems so cool. The author of this next poem seems to agree, since she writes about the bond she shares with her other half.

Twin

My mother's stretch fabric belly
protected us like a T-shirt
on an albino body at the beach.
During our bonding months,
Mom's blue eyes got fixed into our
    sockets,
and her eczema was etched
into our skin.

Our birth left her scarless,
except for stretch marks that I
will take back one day.
My sister's scar and mine

For Real?

Mary-Kate and Ashley Olsen **aren't** actually **identical twins**—they're **fraternal twins** who just happen to look very similar!

is not a broken tree branch;
it is our ears. She hates
that our folds don't separate
like atoms in mitosis.

When she leaves for city
dirt and a new roommate,
I won't have someone
with an identical crooked toe
and oval face
in the same position as mine.

We'll move through different states
spinning on different axes
and time zones. She'll think of me
when she coughs up pollution
and the gunk from steamrollers.
I will think of her when I scratch
my eczema and refuse the stretch
   marks
that have grown on my swinging
   hips.

THE WORD

Mitosis is what happens when **one cell divides into two**, which is what happens in the early stages of identical twin development.

CONSIDER THIS . . .

Not all **celebrity twin sets** are in the public eye. Check out these celebrities with twin siblings:

• Alanis Morissette
  (twin brother)

• Justin Timberlake
  (twin sister)

• Jill Hennessey
  (twin sister)

Sara Moulton, age 19

Read It?

Famous author Anna Quindlen wrote a book called *Siblings*, which contains essays celebrating these special relationships.

Spotlight On ... SIBLINGS

If you have brothers, sisters or both, then you know firsthand that having siblings can be both great and challenging. But a closer look at sibling relationships shows that many of the same things that make it hard about having siblings are also what makes it awesome.

Among the potentially tough things about having a brother or sister around the house are:

- competition for attention from parents
- people making comparisons, both good and bad, about you and your siblings
- sleeping under the same roof, so getting away from them can be hard
- someone is always there to threaten to tattle on you if you screw up

But wait, it's not all bad. There are great things about having siblings:

- When it comes down to it, you know someone always has your back.
- You've got twenty-four-hour access, and if you need them, the bond between blood can be stronger than with friends.

- Siblings have seen you in every situation, good and bad, so you don't have to worry about not being yourself.
- You've got a built-in companion on family vacations.

WHEN I MOVED INTO THE HOUSE I LIVE IN NOW, the people who lived here before decided to take all of the mirrors along with them. Even the bathroom mirrors were gone. Because we were so busy, we didn't get around to buying new mirrors for a couple of weeks. What an odd thing it was to walk around day after day without knowing what I looked like! I soon realized that I wasn't being nearly as self-conscious as usual. I was going makeup-free, and I let my hair air-dry after showers because I couldn't see what I was doing with the blow dryer anyway.

Read It?

The Artist's Way by Julia Cameron is a workbook that provides tools and space for **discovering** your authentic **self**.

When we finally did hang a mirror in the bathroom, I took a good hard look at myself. Had I aged? Had I always looked this way? I couldn't help but feel surprised that the reflection I saw didn't necessarily match what I thought I looked like when the mirror wasn't around.

Just as it can be great to be free from mirrors, sometimes catching a glimpse of our reflection can be a powerful experience and can show us things we never thought we'd see.

My Reflection

I met a girl the other day.
She was different from me
   in many ways.
I know I have met her in
   the past,
But I don't know if our
   friendship will last.
Her hair is different, and she
   doesn't dress the same as before.
I felt like I didn't know who she was anymore.
She left her old friends and joined a new crew.
Once a cute guy came along, she would leave her new crew, too.
Her old friends told her she was being fake.
They didn't know how much they could take.
They tried to prove a point to her, and she shed a tear.
They told her to go and look at herself in a mirror.
When I saw all this happening, I thought how could this be,
This new girl seemed so opposite of me?
But when I looked in the mirror, what did I see?
My reflection! All along this new girl was me.

Alicia Vasquez, age 19

For Real?

The **first mirrors**, used in the Middle Ages, were hand mirrors. People didn't have a chance to **see their whole body** reflected through full-length mirrors until the 1ˢᵗ century AD.

CONSIDER THIS . . .

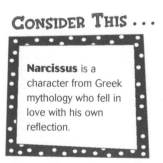

Narcissus is a character from Greek mythology who fell in love with his own reflection.

OUTSIDE THE BOX

Sometimes life gets so crazy that it's hard to take the time to tune in. Are you feeling a little out of sorts? Do you need to reconnect with yourself and get comfortable in your own shoes again? Try some of these ideas:

- Reread your journal or diary. It's amazing to see how clearly you expressed yourself in the pages.
- Flip through old photo albums and reflect on the events captured on film.
- Go for a walk in nature or grab a blanket and a good book and hang out at the park for a day. Sometimes spending quality time alone can remind you of things that make you feel good.
- Come up with a theme song for yourself . . . one that makes you feel strong, powerful, creative and inspired. Then whenever you need a boost, pop in the CD and crank it up.

Seen It?

In the ABC show *Lost,* Korean character Jin develops friendships with everyone else on the island even though he doesn't speak a word of English.

CAN TWO PEOPLE FROM TWO VERY DIFFERENT COUNTRIES, cultures and lifestyles actually be friends? What if they don't even speak the same language? Is there such a thing as a "universal language"? What do you think? If you were traveling abroad and you came across someone who didn't speak English, would you take it as a sign of friendliness if they communicated to you in one of these ways?

- Smiling
- Winking
- Pointing out directions on a map for you
- Offering you something to eat or drink
- Laughing at something silly you did
- Giving you the thumbs-up sign
- Holding open a door for you

The truth is, whether a universal language exists or not, the concept of friendship and friendliness *is* universal.

HOW ABOUT YOU?

Have you ever **communicated nonverbally** with someone you didn't know?

The Friendship Cake

I used to listen only halfheartedly when my parents told me I should be thankful for what I had. My friends were girls who had the same interests in soccer and school as me. We all tried to act like individuals, but let's face it . . . we wore the exact same style of jeans and sweatshirts. In fact, we were all pretty much alike. Things changed when I had the opportunity to go to Africa.

For Real?

Lake Victoria is the second **largest freshwater lake** in the world. Bugala Island is one of a group of eighty-four islands called the Sesse Islands.

After a twenty-one-hour flight, we arrived at our destination—Bugala Island, Uganda, in the middle of Lake Victoria. The eight-mile-long island had only one rutted road. The people there lived in cow-dung huts without running water or electricity. (I won't even describe what the toilets looked like.)

Seen It?

The classic Humphrey Bogart/Katharine Hepburn movie, *The African Queen* (1951), takes place on a river in Uganda.

While on Bugala Island, I had a chance to meet the girl I sponsored through Childcare International, a Christian relief agency. Her name was Annette, and her parents and relatives had died of AIDS. Through the thirty-dollar donation my family made each month, Annette was able to live in a group home and go to school. Annette and I had been writing letters back and forth for some time. I made sure not to write about our house, my closet full of clothes or the big trips we took. Here

For Real?
If you're a teenager, Uganda might be the place for you . . . over half the population is under the age of fifteen!

was a girl my own age who owned only two dresses and one pair of flip-flops. Before we left for our trip, my mom and I thought about buying Annette a backpack. I'm glad that we didn't because I soon saw she had nothing to put in it—no stuffed animals, no boxes of markers . . . no books.

When I first met Annette, I had on my favorite khaki shorts, not knowing that most girls in Uganda seldom wear shorts or pants. She hugged me cautiously—after all, she had never seen a Caucasian girl before. Within five minutes, Annette disappeared into her group home. She returned moments later wearing a faded pair of shorts, trying to look like me. Annette spoke English fairly well, so we could talk, but I panicked. How could I be friends with someone who had never even seen water coming out of a faucet?

Surprisingly, it didn't take long for us to form a friendship. She showed me the room she shared with twenty other orphan girls, who by now were all wearing shorts, too. Annette taught me how to play their jump-rope games, and we played the drums together and did craft projects. I found myself having fun with Annette even though she had never seen a video or eaten at McDonald's. Our life experiences couldn't have been more different, yet there we were . . . hanging out like old friends.

For Real?
If you're traveling and have a hankering for a Big Mac, chances are a **McDonald's** is just down the street. McDonald's can be found in more than **100 countries** worldwide.

Address Book

If you're interested in learning more about **relief** and **development** organizations working in **other countries**, check out some of the links below:

• CARE (*www.care.org*)
• Catholic Relief Services (*www.catholicrelief.org*)
• Childcare International (*www.childcare-intl.org*)
• Save the Children (*www.savethechildren.org*)

On the last night of our trip, the kids there planned a celebration for me. Since they didn't have crepe-paper streamers, they twisted toilet paper along the walls to make decorations. Annette, still wearing her shorts, led the group in singing and dancing. The dancing consisted of shaking the hips back and forth so the grass skirts the girls wore swooshed in a blur of color. The children invited me to join in their dance. Three years of ballet lessons never could have prepared me for what was to come. Trying to mimic their dance, I fell short and resorted to my preschool years of twirling and waving my body wildly to the beating of the drums and chanting of the children. They laughed hysterically at my attempts at African dance.

After the dancing and singing, the director of the home announced a special treat—a frosted cake! He brought out a homemade, one-layer, eight-inch cake. Annette and I cut up the cake, and all 120 kids excitedly waited for the rare treat of sweet cake. I figured the Costco-size sheet cakes were on another table. After all, we had to serve over a hundred kids. Instead, Annette cut the eight-inch cake into smaller and smaller pieces . . . these were really small pieces!

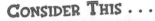

CONSIDER THIS . . .

You don't have to **speak** the **same language** as someone to be his or her friend. Sometimes all it takes to strike up a friendship is a common interest or a shared passion.

I then went around and passed them out, and each child picked up a tiny piece with his or her fingers. Everyone smiled at me as they ate their miniature piece of cake. No one asked for seconds, and no one tried to sneak two pieces. They were simply happy with what they had. Annette made sure I had a piece of cake, too.

For Real?

While there may not be a **Costco** in Uganda or anywhere else in Africa, you can find one in these countries:

• Canada • England
• Japan • Korea • Mexico
• Newfoundland • Taiwan

THE WORD

The word for **celebration** in Uganda's language of Lugunda is **cacanca**.

The next day, while leaving the island, I thought back on that cake. In the United States, my friends would have complained about the tiny piece of cake. "We want a bigger piece! Where's the ice cream?" I found myself happily eating a few cake crumbs next to Annette. It wasn't about the sugar rush. It wasn't about the frosting. It was about the friendship.

Sondra Clark, age 15

WHAT DO YOU THINK?

Do you know the truth about the relationship between people and animals?

1. ⍰ ⍰ Most dogs sleep in their owner's beds every night.

2. ⍰ ⍰ Dolphins are so connected with humans that they come to the rescue when humans at sea are in trouble.

3. ⍰ ⍰ Researchers have been able to teach rhinoceroses a simple form of sign language in order to communicate better with them.

4. ⍰ ⍰ With some primates, it's possible to become accepted as one of them by imitating their behavior.

5. ⍰ ⍰ Parrots are only imitating sounds that they hear when they say things like *Polly wants a cracker*. They don't actually understand what they're saying.

How'd ya do?

1. **True:** More than 60 percent of dogs sleep in their owner's bedrooms!

2. **True:** Dolphins have done everything from leading a ship out of a storm to safety to surrounding a stranded swimmer to protect him from sharks.

3. **False:** Rhinos are actually quite dangerous to humans and will often charge them. It's no wonder when you consider that humans pose the biggest threat to rhinos!

4. **True:** Famous scientist Diane Fossey made her breakthrough discoveries about gorillas by actually imitating their behavior and being accepted into their group in Rwanda.

5. **False:** Some parrots actually use language in context and have a sense of humor to boot!

IF YOU'VE EVER HAD A PET—dog, cat, ferret, mouse, guinea pig, even a snake—then you know that the bond between animals and people can be incredible. I am a dog person. I have a dog named Baxter, and he's a seriously playful white German shepherd who, even as I write this, is taking a nap under my desk. Though he's not the best at giving advice or covering my butt when I screw up, he's always there to love me unconditionally, even when I go out for a run and opt not to take him or forget to feed him a rawhide treat after dinner. I couldn't imagine beginning my day without opening my eyes and being inches away from his big red tongue panting expectantly in my face. I guess one could say that some friendships know no bounds.

HOW ABOUT YOU?

Do you consider an **animal** among your list of **close friends**?

Read It?

Photographer Christopher Ameruouso's book *Pets and Their Celebrities* (2001) features photographs of everyone from Pamela Anderson to Rose McGowan with the animals they love.

Comfort Has Four Legs

A thunderous chorus pounds the
    ground.
Lean, lithe bodies coated with sheens
    of shimmering sweat weave in and
    out of formation.

CONSIDER THIS . . .

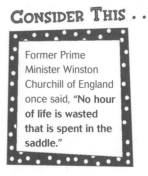

Former Prime Minister Winston Churchill of England once said, **"No hour of life is wasted that is spent in the saddle."**

Golden, gray, black, chestnut, white, spotted and patched;
forming a spectrum superior to any found in the sky.
Rumpled tendrils of mane flare out in the breeze, whipping
like serpents in the dusty wind.
Nostrils dilate and sides heave, drawn-out breaths fuel the
hearts that beat as a herd.
As quickly as they flared into action, the activity ceases.
Tension releases and curiosity takes over as questioning
muzzles investigate who has entered their pasture.
A muffled nicker eases my angst, an insistent nudge knocks
the chip off my shoulder.
Silhouetted on the sun, I lean on a warm, velvety flank,
gleaning comfort from such strength.

*Stephanie Garinger,
age 17*

Seen It?

There are tons of **great movies** about people who have amazing **relationships** with **horses**. Here are just a few:

- *Seabiscuit* (2003)
- *Spirit: Stallion of the Cimarron* (2002)
- *Black Beauty* (1994)
- *The Black Stallion* (1979)

For Real?

Horses living in the wild **sleep for only two to four hours a day** and spend the rest of the time eating. Perhaps this is because they actually exert more energy when they're lying down than when they're standing up!

A Feline Friend

A lot of people say dog is man's best friend. But I know, at least in my case, cat is *woman's* best friend.

My cat, Fargo, got her name when she appeared one fateful day in a patch of woods near our house. We weren't sure how "far" she had to "go" to end up in those woods. Missy, my curious dog, was barking endlessly at something. When my family and I went to see why she was making all the noise, we found a fluffy white kitten, backed up against a tree, shaking nervously. I immediately felt connected to this young, lonely soul. The vet later informed us the kitten was a female, only a few weeks old. We guessed she accidentally wandered away from a nearby farm, but none of our neighbors

Seen It?

The movie *Fargo* (1996) is a **crime thriller** directed by the Coen Brothers that takes place in a small town in Minnesota.

claimed her. After much deliberation, our family decided to keep the stray cat and embark on our first-ever cat-owning adventure. Fargo may have had to "go far" to end up at our house, but she sure didn't have to do too much to make her way into my heart.

Fargo and I quickly became good friends. I visited her frequently in an unused barn on our country property where she made her home. When I wasn't getting acquainted with her in the barn, she found her way to our house and sat outside the door until I came to play with her. We spent a lot of time together during those first few weeks of our relationship. We became friends, and we had no idea how much deeper that friendship would grow.

For Real?

Many more people in the U.S. have cats as pets than dogs. In fact, there are more than **60 million cats as pets** in homes all across America, and almost **40%** of households have at least **one cat**. Are you one of them?

At first my dad was a little leery about letting Fargo inside our house. He envisioned felled curtains and sofas with the stuffing strewn about. But I let Fargo in for short periods of time every now and then, making sure she didn't wreak any havoc. Eventually, after deciding Fargo was a safe cat, my dad gave in, and she was allowed to come in and out of our house as she pleased. After that, I found Fargo inside almost *all* the time. When she wasn't exploring the house on her own, she was hanging out in my room with me, playing, reading or cuddling with me for a nap.

No sooner was Fargo welcomed into our family than I was welcomed into hers. One cool, spring morning about a year after Fargo first came into our lives, I ran down to the barn to refill her food and water before I had to catch the bus to school. Not only did I find Fargo lying peacefully on her blanket, but also four tiny balls of fur kneading milk from their mother! Unbeknownst to me, Fargo had given birth in the middle of the night. This was a significant moment in our relationship. Now I, who had in a sense become Fargo's mother, was not the only "person" in this once-stray cat's life. Fargo had her own children. She, too, was a mother. Not having much experience with

Address Book

If you're interested in **adopting a cat,** check out your local Petco. They hold their **National Pet Adoption Days** and other programs to put people and pets together. Go to *www.petco.org.*

cats and kittens, I didn't want to intrude or harm the new-borns in any way. But Fargo let me approach her new kittens, and I gave each of them a soft rub. I knew then that this would be an adventure Fargo and I would share

HOW ABOUT YOU?

Have you ever had a **stray** animal come into your life? How did it affect you?

together. I would help Fargo raise her kittens, not just as a friend, but as a part of her family.

Six years have passed since I first befriended Fargo. Right now, she is snoozing on my bed just as she did the first time she was allowed in our house. Our friendship has grown since those early days. Together, we watched other loving families adopt two of her kittens because my family couldn't keep them for our own (as much as we wanted to). We've made friends with other cats my family has adopted throughout the years. Fargo has even moved with us two times to different homes. We've helped each other settle into new surroundings.

Every so often, you'll find Fargo on my lap, purring and gazing thoughtfully into my eyes, as I gaze into hers. It's at moments like these that I know taking in Fargo was a deci-sion I'll always be happy my family made. That look in her eyes as she looks into mine is a simple thank-you. But Fargo is the one who deserves the thanks. She has shown me what it might be like to be a mother, a sister and a grandmother. Most of all, she's shown me a very special friendship.

Ruth Young, age 15

HAS A FRIEND EVER BEEN TOO BUSY to spend time with you because he had plans with his "other friend" . . . his *basketball?*

Or maybe you've turned down plans to go to a party because you had a very important meeting with your *journal.* I know that I've skipped out on social plans because my *running shoes* needed to bond with me.

HOW ABOUT YOU?

Do you have any **inanimate "friends"** that you enjoy spending time with?

So, can inanimate objects really be friends? I think so. Think of all the time we spend with things like our pillows, cell phones and, in the case of this next author, musical instruments. And as you'll read in this next poem, sometimes the objects that are a part of our lives are more like us than we might think.

Cello

Sometimes your friends
Are the most unusual people.
My friend is the cello.
It relates to me
In some odd ways.

The cello I play is deeply
    dented
Like me.

For Real?

You probably know that the **cello**, a member of the **violin family**, is made out of wood. But did you know that the **bow** used to play the cello is partially made out of the hair from a **horse's tail**?

All the pain I have gone
   through
Leaves invisible scars
That will never disappear.

When the eye first
   glances at the cello,
It sees a bold, strong
   instrument.
Instantly, the mind
   thinks
It will never crumble,
That it always stands up
   when it's in pain.

CONSIDER THIS . . .

Playing an **instrument** isn't just a way to kill time. There are tons of **benefits!** Here are a few:

• builds confidence and self-esteem
• develops memory skills
• reduces stress
• increases self-discipline, which will help with school
• allows you to impress your friends
• develops coordination of your body, ear and intellect
• presents opportunities to meet people
• stays with you for your whole life

The eye doesn't see, though,
That inside
The cello is really a small, tender mouse
That possesses a mellow voice
And that sobs in grief
When hurt.

The cello and I share some qualities,
Yet, we are both as different
As white and red.
But when mixed together,
We create a gorgeous color.

Crystal Mendoza, age 11

Address Book

For a really cool Web site where you can **sample** different musical **instruments** and even write your own minuet, check out the New York Philharmonic Kidzone at *www.nyphilkids.org/main. phtml.*

WHERE DO YOU STAND?

Do you know the benefits of having "friendships" with things other than people? What would you be more likely to do if . . .

your friend blew off your plans for Saturday night at the last minute?

- Sit home and sulk   (1 point)
- Dig into a good book   (2 points)

you're really upset about something that happened in school, and you need to blow off steam?

- Call a friend   (1 point)
- Shoot some hoops   (2 points)

you were stuck inside on a rainy afternoon with no one to hang with?

- Reach for the remote   (1 point)
- Grab the guitar   (2 points)

your mom asks you to walk to the library to return some books for her?

- Go it solo   (1 point)
- Grab the leash and bring Fido   (2 points)

the phone is ringing, but you're in the middle of writing in your journal?

- Shelve the book   (1 point)
- Take a message   (2 points)

Add up your points:

5–7 = Keep your eyes open . . .
        you might be missing out on
        some great friendships!
8–10 = You've got unusual friends
        everywhere!

WHEN I WAS NINETEEN, I spent the summer volunteer teaching in a summer school for low-income kids in Mexico. I had to fly from my small hometown in Pennsylvania to San Diego, where I would meet up with other kids from the program, and we'd head south of the border together.

When I stepped aboard the US Airways plane, I was full of excitement as well as a little fear of the unknown. It was my first time flying by myself, and this added to my anxious mood. As I squeezed over the woman in the aisle seat to get to the window, I caught a quick glimpse of her. She was about thirty-five, African-American, wearing cool, hip clothes and funky glasses, and she had a smile that beamed genuine warmth. She must have sensed my nervousness, because soon after the plane took off, she started up a conversation with me.

In no time, this woman and I were yakking it up like two long-lost friends. Talking with her was so effortless, something I found surprising because of our age difference. She treated me with respect and was genuinely interested in the things I was doing. She was also involved in working with youth and had just started an organization working with kids in Boston. We had more in common than I could believe.

The five-and-a-half-hour flight flew by, and next thing I knew, we were bidding farewell next to the baggage claim. She handed me a card with her name and address, hugged me good-bye and wished me luck on my upcoming venture. I hugged her back and walked out to the sidewalk to find my ride, a smile glued to my face. What a great way to start off my adventure!

HOW ABOUT YOU?

Have you ever **made a friend** while on a **flight, bus, subway** or some other form of public transportation?

Read It?

In the Young Adult novel *Refugees* by Catherine Stine, a young girl who runs away from California strikes up an unusual friendship with a boy who's fled Afghanistan.

You probably won't be surprised to learn that I never again spoke with this wonderful woman I met on the plane. I went on with my summer, and I can only assume she returned to her new organization and poured her heart into it as she planned. But despite the fact that our paths haven't crossed since, I know that on that day, on that flight, I made a friend.

Directory Assistance

They say that if you have one friend throughout your entire lifetime, you're lucky. That's not even close to true. Parents just say that to make their kids feel better when they get left out of something. You're going to make and lose a ton of friends throughout the course of your life, and if you don't, you've never lived or you smell or something. Sure, there will be one or two who stick with you through thick and thin, hard times and good, ugly haircuts and bad shirts. But friends like that are the exceptions. You want to make a friend? Some of the best people you'll ever meet are the ones you think the least about. Like your barber. Or your bus driver. Or, in my case, my local Directory Assistance operator.

For Real?

The first **telephone operators** had the job of connecting the caller with the person they were trying to phone. Until 1895, these operators answered the phone by saying, **"Well, are you there?"** as opposed to **"Number please?"**

We met on a Saturday night sometime in the middle of June when I was all by myself at home. I was feeling particularly lonely because, well, it was a Saturday night sometime in the middle of June, and I was all by myself at home. My regular friends were all out doing something enjoyable and, somehow, in the midst of all their fun, it had slipped their minds to invite me. *No problem,* I told myself. I grabbed the remote. The television has always been a friend. Not once have I ever seen it having a good time without me. I pressed the "On" button. Static. The cable guys were working down the street and must have cut a line. Awesome.

It was nine at night. My friends were out, I was alone, and the TV wasn't working. I didn't know what to do. Sleeping was out of the question—I wasn't tired, and it was too early anyway. Going out and finding my friends without having been invited would have made me look desperate. For a minute I considered getting my old action figures out of the attic. Then I saw the phone—a direct link to human contact. I picked it up without thinking and dialed the first number that came to mind: Directory Assistance.

For Real?
The **inventor** of the **telephone**, Alexander Graham Bell, never had a chance to speak to his wife on the phone . . . she was **deaf!**

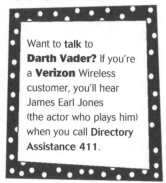

CONSIDER THIS . . .

Want to **talk** to **Darth Vader?** If you're a **Verizon** Wireless customer, you'll hear James Earl Jones (the actor who plays him) when you call **Directory Assistance 411**.

It rang twice, and the computerized male voice asked me to state my city. I did. Then it asked me what number I needed. I didn't need anybody's number.

"Oh," I said, "I just wanted to talk to somebody." There was an awkward silence.

An operator picked up. "I'm sorry, sir, what was that?" Her voice was really southern. Sort of a cute southern sound, though, like the voice of that girl on *The Beverly Hillbillies* who used a rope as a belt. She sounded really nice.

Seen It?

In the comedy *Swingers* (1996), actor Jon Favreau's character screws up his chances with a **crush** by calling her answering machine repeatedly and leaving desperate messages.

"I just wanted someone to talk to, ma'am." When I realized how pathetic that must have sounded, it was too late.

"Someone to talk to?" she asked in that sweet voice of hers. She seemed amused.

"Yeah."

"Okay. What about?" That caught me off guard. I didn't expect anyone to actually *want* to talk to me. I thought they would have hung up. It was more of a prank call than anything. Then again, I didn't expect the operator to have such a nice voice, either. The whole phone call was somewhat of a shock. But hey, it beat loneliness. So we talked for a couple hours.

Her name was Alex, and she was twenty-nine and engaged. She had blonde hair and blue eyes. Her fiancé was a thirty-something-year-old rich guy who was on a business trip in Japan and had been there for the past week. She missed him pretty badly. She said she felt really lonely at the moment. I told her I knew how she felt. She said it was surely nice having someone to talk to about it. I agreed. Her job stunk. She said it was really boring. She didn't even need the money anyway. She was marrying into money. Turns out we both loved popcorn shrimp, and when it came to movies, neither of us liked dramatic ones. She wanted to have three kids with her soon-to-be husband. I said three sounded like a good number to me. She asked me how old I was. I told her twenty-eight. She didn't believe me. So I told her the truth—fourteen. She told me that our phone call was probably costing my parents a lot of money by the minute. I said I didn't care. She laughed.

READER/CUSTOMER CARE SURVEY

We care about your opinions! Please take a moment to fill out our online Reader Survey at **http://survey.hcibooks.com**. As a **"THANK YOU"** you will receive a **VALUABLE INSTANT COUPON** towards future book purchases as well as a **SPECIAL GIFT** available only online! Or, you may mail this card back to us and we will send you a copy of our exciting catalog with your valuable coupon inside.

First Name		MI.	Last Name	
Address				City
State	Zip			Email

1. Gender
- ❑ Female   ❑ Male

2. Age
- ❑ 8 or younger
- ❑ 9-12   ❑ 13-16
- ❑ 17-20   ❑ 21-30
- ❑ 31+

3. Did you receive this book as a gift?
- ❑ Yes   ❑ No

4. How did you find out about the book?
- ❑ Friend
- ❑ School
- ❑ Parent
- ❑ Online
- ❑ Store Display
- ❑ Teen Magazine
- ❑ Interview/Review

5. Where do you usually buy books?
(please choose one)
- ❑ Bookstore
- ❑ Online
- ❑ Book Club/Mail Order
- ❑ Price Club (Sam's Club, Costco's, etc.)
- ❑ Retail Store (Target, Wal-Mart, etc.)

6. What magazines do you like to read? *(please choose one)*
- ❑ Teen People
- ❑ Seventeen
- ❑ YM
- ❑ Cosmo Girl
- ❑ Rolling Stone
- ❑ Teen Ink
- ❑ Christian Magazines

7. What books do you like to read? *(please choose one)*
- ❑ Fiction
- ❑ Self-help
- ❑ Reality Stories/Memoirs
- ❑ Sports
- ❑ Series Books (Chicken Soup, Fearless, etc.)

8. What attracts you most to a book?
(please choose one)
- ❑ Title
- ❑ Cover Design
- ❑ Author
- ❑ Content

TAPE IN MIDDLE; DO NOT STAPLE

BUSINESS REPLY MAIL

FIRST-CLASS MAIL PERMIT NO 45 DEERFIELD BEACH, FL

POSTAGE WILL BE PAID BY ADDRESSEE

Chicken Soup for the Teenage Soul
The Real Deal Friends
3201 SW 15th Street
Deerfield Beach FL 33442-9875

|ₗₗₗ||ₗₗₗₗ||ₗₗₗₗₗ|ₗₗₗₗₗₗ|ₗₗₗₗₗₗₗₗₗ|ₗₗₗₗₗ|

FOLD HERE

Comments

Do you have your own Chicken Soup story
that you would like to send us?
Please submit at: **www.chickensoup.com**

She thought I was pretty funny. That made me feel good.

We got off the phone around eleven when my parents got home. The two hours that we talked to each other went by fast. When I hung up, I wasn't exactly sure what had just happened. But I knew I'd had a good Saturday night, thanks to her.

So a couple of days later, I called her back. We talked some more. Our phone calls became more and more frequent. Pretty soon, we were talking twice a day. My parents thought I had a new girlfriend and told me I should invite her over to the house. They were puzzled when I told them that her fiancé probably wouldn't like that. They understood when they got the phone bill at the end of the month.

I had to say good-bye to Alex. I miss her whenever I get lonely. But it's been two years, and she's probably moved somewhere with her fiancé by now. I hope he's good to her. It was a great friendship, even if it didn't last long. It's like I said—friends come in all shapes and sizes. And voices, I guess.

Michael Wassmer, age 16

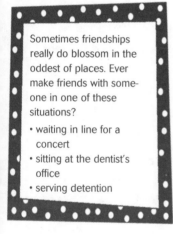

CONSIDER THIS . . .

Sometimes friendships really do blossom in the oddest of places. Ever make friends with someone in one of these situations?

• waiting in line for a concert
• sitting at the dentist's office
• serving detention

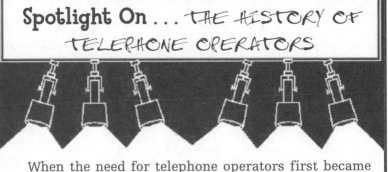

Spotlight On . . . THE HISTORY OF TELEPHONE OPERATORS

When the need for telephone operators first became evident in the early 1900s, the job was usually reserved for teenage boys, mostly because they would do the work for very little pay. But teen boys were soon replaced with women since they found that women were more patient with callers and were happy to do the work because there weren't many job options for women at that time. Here are some interesting (and shocking!) facts about the first women telephone operators:

- Women operators had to be between seventeen and twenty-six years old.
- All women operators had to look and dress "prim and proper" and have long arms so they could reach the switchboard.
- African-American and Jewish women could not be hired as telephone operators.
- The first women telephone operators earned the tiny salary of seven dollars a week.
- If a woman operator got married, she was forced to quit.
- Early women telephone operators didn't just connect calls—they gave weather reports, election results, traffic reports, etc.

Take the Quiz:
ARE YOU OPEN TO UNUSUAL FRIENDSHIPS

1. You weren't so sure how happy you were when your parents told you they were expecting another child four years ago, and now your four-year-old little sister just thinks you're the coolest thing since *Blue's Clues*. She wants to do absolutely everything you do. How do you cope?

   ___ A. You couldn't be more annoyed with this little person who wants to look, dress and act like you. You post a sign on your door saying, "No one under the age of ten allowed!"

   ___ B. You think your little sister's devotion to you is kind of cool, and you find yourself enjoying the time you spend together more than you could imagine. She may not be able to give you advice, but her wide-eyed view of the world gives you perspective.

   ___ C. You like being a big sister and all, but you can handle only so much "little sis time" every day. Even though you find yourself laughing a lot when hanging out with her, you're not ready to go out of your way to do so.

2. Your mom invites a colleague and his family over for dinner, telling you they have a son your age with whom you'll surely get along. But no one warned you ahead of time that he's blind, and you're thrown a little off guard. What do you do?

   ___ A. You're nervous, but decide to treat the boy like you would anyone else, while trying to be sensitive to his different needs. Instead of dictating what the two of you will do, you ask him what kind of things he's into and go from there.

   ___ B. You are unsure how to act around the blind boy since you've never met anyone with a disability like this before. You're both surprised

and relieved at the same time when he says he wants to watch
The O.C. with you—now you won't have to try to entertain him.

___ C. You escape to your bedroom as soon as dessert is cleared, telling
your folks you've got a killer homework assignment to tackle.
You've never hung out with a blind person before and figure a
friendship would be too much work.

3. A big blizzard has hit, and you're stuck inside with no friends,
no electricity, no nothing. Things won't get back to normal for
at least a day, and you're at a loss about how to spend your
time. How do you handle it?

___ A. You see this as the perfect opportunity to work on one of the creative projects you've got in mind. With no distractions like the
phone, computer or TV, you'll be able to finish the handmade
scrapbook you started last month.

___ B. Being cut off from the outside world is your worst nightmare! You
begrudgingly play board games with your family by candlelight
and escape to the solace of your room as soon as you can.

___ C. It's been a while since you've been forced to entertain yourself,
so you find yourself bored out of your mind until you remember
you got a novel for your birthday that you haven't touched yet.
You decide to use the time to dig in to a new book.

4. Your wacky aunt, whom you refer to as "crazy Aunt Shelley,"
calls you up out of the blue and says she wants to start spending more time with you, starting this weekend. "Let's have
lunch!" she says. How do you respond?

___ A. You reluctantly agree to grab lunch with your aunt on Saturday,
but you make sure she knows you have plans later that afternoon,
so if it doesn't work out, you have an excuse to ditch out early.

___ B. The thought of hanging out with your aunt for an entire afternoon
isn't a good one. What if you have nothing in common? What if it's
all awkward and strange? You tell her that you've got plans this
weekend and push it off for another time.

___ C. You're flattered that crazy Aunt Shelley wants to spend time with you and jump in full force. If she's taking an interest in you, she's gotta be cool, right?

5. You're not much of a dog person, so you are confused as to why a stray dog has followed you all the way home from field hockey practice. By the time you get to your front door, he's still by your side, looking up with those big brown eyes. What do you do?

___ A. You go inside and leave the dog on the front porch. Even if it is cute, you just don't connect with animals, so there's no point in leading him on. Besides, he'll eventually get bored and move on to another house.

___ B. You wonder if this dog has found you for a reason. After all, why did he choose *you* to go home with? You bring out a bowl of water and sit on the front porch with the dog, getting to know him a little better until your parents get home and you can figure out what to do.

___ C. You are trying not to get involved, but you can't help but melt when the dog looks at you so sweetly. You call a friend who loves dogs and ask her if she's interested in keeping this dog.

Add 'em up! Give yourself the following points:

1. a = 10, b = 30, c = 20; 2. a = 30, b = 20, c = 10; 3. a = 30, b = 10, c = 20; 4. a = 20, b = 10, c = 30; 5. a = 10, b = 30, c = 20.

Look below to find out how open you are to making friends who aren't what you expect:

50–70 points = You're more closed off than an old dog who refuses to learn new tricks. The problem is, if you don't stay open to new people, you'll never know what you're missing.

80–120 points = You're fairly accepting of others and know that friends can come where you least expect them, but sometimes you forget and fall into your old patterns of going through life with blinders on.

130–150 points = You are as open as can be, and this is a great thing because often the friendships that come along when we least expect them become the most powerful ones in our lives.

CHAPTER 5

BLURRY LINES

C an boys and girls be just friends, or does it always get messy when opposite-sex friendship is involved? And what if a friendship does turn into more . . . can it end happily ever after? Or if it goes bad, does that mean the end of the friendship, too? This chapter looks at the complicated issues that come up when love and friendship mix.

STRETCH LIMOS. WRIST CORSAGES. A cheesy DJ. Hair that defies gravity. Pictures taken by a strange guy in a bad tux who prompts you to smile by encouraging you to say the word "cheesecake." Is there any doubt that I'm talking about that four-letter-word . . . PROM?

What is it about prom that conjures up such emotional responses? People usually have some sort of strong opinion about prom and all its traditions. Do you fit into one of these categories?

CONSIDER THIS . . .

Think **prom** isn't a **big deal** for teens? Here are just a few of the popular movies with prom scenes:
• *She's All That* (1999)
• *10 Things I Hate About You* (1999)
• *Not Another Teen Movie* (2001)
• *Pretty in Pink* (1986)
• *Better Off Dead* (1985)

1. You've been dreaming about prom your whole life and know it will be the penultimate experience of your high-school life.
2. You act as if you couldn't care less about prom, but secretly harbor a fantasy of it being a dreamy night.
3. You figure you'll go because everyone else is, but you're not going to get all into it.
4. You boycott the prom and decide to stay at home and watch reruns of *CSI* instead.

I think I fell into number two of the above. I definitely wasn't a girly girl, so therefore couldn't act as if prom was a big deal to me. And it's a good thing, too, because neither the junior nor senior prom that I went to was a dreamy fantasy date. In fact, junior year I went with a boy I had been dating, but by the time prom came around, we were no longer a couple. Boy, was *that* awkward. Senior year, I went with another former boyfriend, but this time it was clear we were going as friends, a controversial decision among my group to say the least. The notion of prom being a thing between friends is pondered in this next essay.

"Friends with Benefits," Prom-Style

My knees shook inside my favorite pair of "skinny jeans." I took a deep breath, my courage fortified by a Mountain Dew sugar high. And then I did it. I walked right up to my high-school crush and said five simple words: "Hey, wanna go to prom?"

Then the unthinkable happened. "Yeah," he said. "I'd love to."

Pause. Awkward smile. "But . . ."

Oh, no. Not *but*. Please, not *but!*

". . . but I already promised to go with one of my friends."

> **For Real?**
> **"Prom"** comes from the word "promenade." In the 1500s, a promenade was another word for a walk. By the end of the 1800s, people were using the word to mean a formal ball or dance.

Super duper dandy. My heart—and ego—deflated like a popped prom balloon. I mumbled something along the lines of, "Oh-yeah-that's-fine-totally-understand-just-thought-I'd-ask-you-know-ha-ha-okay-well-bye-now-I'm-gonna-move-to-a-convent-far-far-away-and-become-a-nun."

My friend gave me a "that's his loss" consolation speech. "Whatever," I said. "It probably worked out for the best. It's hard to dance in a habit, anyway." My friend laughed because she thought I was joking.

THE WORD

A **habit** is the piece of **clothing** that **nuns wear**.

In all seriousness, though, I was angry at my crush's so-called "friend." I mean, everyone knows you don't go to prom with a friend. Prom is supposed to be a perfect romantic night. Doesn't she read teen magazines?

I'm a forgiving person, though. I forgave this friend, whoever she was, for her lack of prom know-how and mentally prepared myself for a Home Alone Prom Night Party of One. I compiled a list of chick flicks to rent, bought the ingredients for my mom's triple-chocolate fudge brownies and searched the Internet for nearby convents.

And then the unthinkable happened . . . *again*. One of my guy "friends" asked *me* to prom.

* * *

After mulling it over for about two-tenths of a second, I, of course, said, "Yes." Going to prom with a friend, I figured, was better than not going to prom at all. Besides, I don't like to bake, and I'd watched *How to Lose a Guy in Ten Days* fourteen times already. Plus, I still harbored a secret fantasy that once my crush saw me in my gorgeous dress with my perfect hair and flawless makeup, he would realize that I was the girl he was supposed to be with, and we would dance the night away in each other's arms . . .

Seen It?

Hilary Duff goes from geek to prom princess in the romantic comedy *A Cinderella Story* (2004).

Yeah, right.

(In case you're wondering, agreeing to go to prom with *my* friend does not make me a hypocrite. I specifically told my friend that if another girl asked him to go in a more-than-friends way, he had my blessing to go with her instead. I would understand—*boy would I!* But nobody asked him. So that was that.)

* * *

Surprisingly, I didn't spend the days leading up to prom worried and anxious that something would go terribly wrong, that I'd get a huge pimple on my nose, and that my date wouldn't have a good time. Even if disaster struck, I knew it wouldn't ruin the night.

Whatever happened, I would have fun because I would be with my friends . . . and I always have fun with my friends.

For Real?

Proms are a **big** business. The average teen spends more than **$600** on prom, and it's more than a three-billion-dollar-a-year business!

My fellow girl prom-mites and I got together on the day of the big event and gave each other manicures and pedicures and help with hair and makeup. (In my opinion, getting ready for prom is one of the best parts of the night!) Then we met up with our guy friend "dates" at a backyard barbeque. We ate hamburgers and french fries, played charades and Twister, took tons of pictures, and even watched *Finding Nemo*. There was no forced small talk or awkward gaps of silence because I was with a big group of friends. And believe me, we never have a problem finding a topic to discuss. It was already turning out to be one of the most fun nights of my life . . . and the actual dance hadn't even begun yet!

When it comes to dancing, doing it with friends can have benefits—like not having to feel self-conscious. We waltzed; we jigged; we swing-danced; we did the robot. A little wild, sure; a little immature, maybe. A lot of fun? Definitely! *When else*, I thought, *will I get the chance to do the funky chicken in a formal dress? I'll have the rest of my life to act—and dance—like an adult. Why not take advantage of my youthful immaturity while I can get away with it?*

On the other hand, if I had gone to prom with my crush, I would have been one of those couples waiting around for someone else to kick up the party a notch, worried about making a fool of myself, worried about looking "stupid," worried about what others were thinking instead of what I *should* be worried about—having fun.

Instead of spending a fortune on expensive picture packages, my buddies and I took along disposable cameras and snapped pictures throughout the dance. Instead of stiff, formal portraits, we were left with rolls and rolls of fun, candid, wacky, real-life photos. Plus, friends generally have a much longer shelf life than crushes or boyfriends. I helped pass out prom pictures when they came in a few weeks after the dance. One girl stormed up, grabbed her $90 picture packet and promptly ripped it to pieces. I stood there in bewilderment until her friend explained, "Her boyfriend broke up with her a week ago." The dumpee looked over and said, "Yeah, I hate his guts." What wonderful prom memories she must have!

*　*　*

My friends and I, however, were left with priceless prom memories—even if they didn't include goodnight kisses on front stoops or confessions of undying love. Instead, we went out for ice cream, our boy *friends* went home, and my fellow girl prom-mites and I had a sleepover. It was the perfect PG ending to a wonderful night.

And, oh yeah, in case you're wondering whatever happened to my crush . . . I saw him briefly at the dance and said "hello." He seemed to be having fun with his "friend" as well, for which I was happy.

HOW ABOUT YOU?

Would you go to **prom** with a **friend**?

We ended up becoming good friends ourselves. In my yearbook he wrote, "I'm sorry I didn't go to prom with you." But the funny thing is, I'm not . . . sorry, that is. Looking back, I ended up having a much better time *not* going to prom with my crush than I probably would have if we *had* gone together.

I did the unthinkable. I went to prom with a *friend*. And, believe me, it had a lot of benefits.

Dallas Nicole Woodburn, age 17

Spotlight On ... WHEN ROMANCE GETS IN THE WAY OF FRIENDSHIPS

Have you ever heard the saying "boyfriends and girl-friends come and go, but friendships are forever"? It's a nice saying, but in reality, it's not 100 percent true. In fact, some boyfriends and girlfriends do last forever, while some friendships fade away.

No matter how you feel about the above quote, the truth is, when a friend becomes romantically interested in someone, whether it's just a crush or a full-on relation-ship, it can put a strain on the friendship. Suddenly, time spent between friends comes second to time spent with a boyfriend or girlfriend. Sure, they still want to hang out with you, but only if their crush isn't available. Or maybe your friend is heartbroken by a crush, and nothing you do can cheer her up. The things the two of you used to enjoy together just suddenly don't seem as fun.

While you can't control how your friend handles it when he or she is in a relationship or crushing hard on someone, here are some ways to make sure that when you're in that position, you don't jeopardize your friendships:

- Keep balance in your life . . . there's enough time to hang out with your friends and your crush separately.
- Continue doing things with your friend that are unique to the two of you.
- Don't blow off your friend at the last minute if a better offer comes along from a boyfriend or girlfriend.
- Talk to a sibling or parent and ask them if they think you're keeping things in perspective. Sometimes when you're "in it," it's hard to see what's really going on.

MAYBE IT'S SOMETHING HE SAID IN A LATE-NIGHT PHONE CALL. Maybe it's the *way* it was said. Or maybe it's just a look from her, a smile . . . a twinkle in her eyes that wasn't there before. Or maybe it's *you*. Maybe you're the one who can't maintain eye contact for long because your cheeks start to get all blotchy and red. Or you begin second-guessing everything you say to your "friend," wondering if he or she took it the wrong way, wondering why you said it in the first place, how you could have said something so *dumb*.

I'm talking about the moment a friendship starts to potentially become something more. The emotions involved run deep—excitement, fear, anxiety, hopefulness. Until we find out how the other person feels, everything is a little weird. But is it worth it to take the plunge and spill the beans about your true feelings?

Seen It?

Remember when Joey and Rachel started liking each other on *Friends*? After **trying** out the boyfriend/girlfriend thing, they decided they were **better off** being just friends.

Just Friends

Here's the story of a guy,
Who learns that no matter how hard you try,
"Best friends forever" means just that.

It all began one normal day,
When everything was fine.
The new girl sat down next to me,
Her heart beat close to mine.

Read It?

Hailey Abbott's book
Summer Boys tells the tale
of a triangle of friends who
are crushing on each other.

We often said "hello" and "hi,"
Talked about things so dumb.
I never would have guessed then that
Such good friends we'd become.

Together we talked and laughed,
We knew what the other liked and desired.
She was funny, pretty and smart,
And that was everything I admired.

"Best friends 'til the end" we promised,
And soon the months passed.
You grew on me, I grew on you?
Time flew by so fast.

I took the plunge, I held my breath,
I meant those fateful words.
You said, "Can't we just be friends?"
But "no" is what I heard.

My heart was crushed and torn in half,
It was the moment that I'd dreaded.

You left me with no
other choice,
So just friends we'll
stay instead.

Matthew Chee,
age 15

WHERE DO YOU STAND?

Would you approach friendships differently if you had a significant other? Would
you ever . . .

start hanging out with your new S.O.'s
friends instead of your own so that they like
you, too?

- I just might   (0 points)
- I'm not sure   (1 point)
- Not on your life   (2 points)

spill the beans about a secret between you
and your BFF because you wanted your
S.O. to know you trusted him or her?

- I just might   (0 points)
- I'm not sure   (1 point)
- Not on your life   (2 points)

stop turning to your friends with your problems b ecause you have a serious S.O. to
go to instead?

- I just might   (0 points)
- I'm not sure   (1 point)
- Not on your life   (2 points)

cancel longstanding plans with your BFF
because something with your S.O. came up
that you'd rather do?

- I just might   (0 points)
- I'm not sure   (1 point)
- Not on your life   (2 points)

start acting differently, and when your friends
call you on it, tell them they're just jealous?

- I just might   (0 points)
- I'm not sure   (1 point)
- Not on your life   (2 points)

Add up your points:
0–3 = You change like the weather.
4–7 = Depends on the S.O.
8–10 = Your feet are on the ground.

OUTSIDE THE BOX

Have you confessed your romantic feelings to someone only to be told he or she wants to only be "just friends?" If you ever find yourself in that situation again, here are some great ways to respond to keep your cool:

- *"Oh, I was just rehearsing a monologue for a play audition. I didn't mean it!"*
- *"Phew, that's a relief. I said that only because I thought you felt that way and, I wanted to spare your feelings."*
- *"April Fools!" (Note: This one really only works one day out of the year!)*

I USED TO KEEP A JOURNAL AS A TEEN, full of the words of famous poets like Carl Sandburg and e.e. cummings, my own questionable attempts at poetry, and some other miscellaneous ponderings on this or that. Stuffed between the back pages are some letters from middle school that I just can't bear to get rid of. Even now as I go back and reread the letters—from friends, boyfriends, want-to-be boyfriends and soon-to-be ex-boyfriends—I'm mesmerized by how tangible and gritty they are.

There's something so personal about reading someone else's words in her own scrawled handwriting, knowing she hand-picked the pen or pencil she used, chose a certain type of paper or stationery to write on, and then let her heart spill out onto the page. In this day and age of cyber *everything,* a good, old-fashioned letter can be a powerful way to express your emotions, good and bad, to someone else.

For Real?

The poet **e.e. cummings** is known for **not** using capital letters when others would, even using lower case "i" when referring to himself.

OUTSIDE THE BOX

Is there anything better than coming home from school to find a hand-addressed envelope with your name on it waiting in the mailbox? How cool is it that someone took the time to write to you, scrounge up an envelope, stick on a stamp and pop it into the mail? But to get letters, you have to send them, too. Here are some ideas for getting your own letter-writing going:

- Write monthly updates to your grandparents . . . they'll love hearing from you, and they'll be sure to write back!
- Write letters to a friend who's away for the summer and ask him to do the same.
- Find a penpal from another country and start up a correspondence. The insight you'll gain will be amazing!

Can't Fall in Love with a Friend

June 2, 2004

My love,
I don't know if I'm ready to get over you . . . if I'm ready to
   move on,
All I know is that I love you, and I've loved you for so long.
There are other takers for my heart,
But getting over you will tear it apart.
I wanted you, I wanted you so very bad,

When I knew I couldn't have you, it
    made me really sad.
And now that your love goes to her,
    it's causing my emotions to stir,
It's like I have a disease, and you're
    the only cure.
But I know she loves you, and I won't interfere,
I will just sit back and watch my whole world disappear.
We're good friends, but I want to be something more.
I want you to look at me and love me more than her.
Some people are addicted to drugs, but I'm addicted to you,
I wish you could know how I feel, I wish you only knew.

Seen It?

In the period piece
Dangerous Liasons
(1988), Michelle Pfieffer
plays a woman who
dies of a **broken heart**.

June 16, 2004

My love,
I need you more than air,
You with her? It's just not fair.
My only wish is to be with you,
But how can I if she's with you, too?
When I told you that I loved you, I
    thought everything would change,
I'm sorry . . . I forgot that love and
    hearts cannot rearrange.
When I told you that I loved
    you, I thought you'd drop
    everything and run to me,
Maybe even someday you'd get
    on one knee and say,
"Baby, I love you, will you
    marry me?"

Address Book

To hook up with a **penpal**
from **another country,**
check out International
Pen Friends at *www.ipf*
europe.com/ipfenglish.htm.

THE WORD

Addiction is a psychological or
physiological **compulsion** to do
something. Many people who are
addicted say their behavior is out
of their control.

I need to stop dreaming and open my eyes.
You and I, we will never be,
Why is it taking me so long to see?
You love her, and you don't love me.

July 2, 2004

My love,
I'm starting to see,
That we will never be.
I don't know if I should give
 up hope and stop trying,
Or if I should never stop
 and keep on crying.
My mind and heart ache
 when I see you together,
I don't know what to do
 when you say that you'll be with her forever.
I want to hate you so I can move on,
But I have been at this crazy game for way too long.
I guess this is how my cards have been dealt,
Me not with you, but with someone else.

HOW ABOUT YOU?

Have you ever **written** someone a **love letter** and then **regretted** passing it on to them?

Amanda O'Connell, age 14

THERE IS THIS MOVIE I LOVE called *Some Kind of Wonderful*. Eric Stoltz and Mary Stuart Masterson play best friends, except Mary is completely in love with Eric. And, of course, he hasn't a clue. It's not until the very end that he starts to put it together, goes back over events in his head and realizes that she was trying to tell him all along how she felt. He was just too blind to see it. I won't tell you how it ends . . . you'll have to rent it to find out.

Being a big fan of romance movies, I used to wonder how Eric could be so dense. I mean, hey, everyone else knew how she felt. Why was he so blind to it? I used to wonder, that is, until I was in the same position a few years later when a friend confessed that he had serious feelings for me and completely blew me away. I had been so wrapped up in my own drama that I never even considered what might be going on with him. Wanna find out how that one ended? Rent the movie . . .

OUTSIDE THE BOX

Do you think a friend might be crushing on you? Here are some signs to look for:

- Keeps eye contact longer than usual
- Looks for excuses to grab your hand or make other physical contact
- Blushes when talking with you
- Sounds nervous on the phone
- His friends tease him whenever you're around
- He suddenly starts trying to look extra nice whenever you hang out

A Changing Season

I went to his soccer games, and he went to my shows. I thought I could count on him, and he could count on me. That's how best friends work. And that's exactly what Chris was—my best friend. At least, I thought he was. With his short blond hair and daydreaming blue eyes, he was my stability. That's *was*, not *is*.

CONSIDER THIS . . .

Until recently, teen girls who wore **makeup** in **Japan** were considered **juvenile** delinquents.

Our friendship was easy to figure out—not much was left to the imagination. Everyone knew we were the best of friends. If you couldn't find Chris, he was likely with me, and vice versa. He always had a girlfriend, and I was always flirting with his friends. I never cared if my shirt was wrinkled or I wasn't wearing makeup around him. I mean, it was just Chris. In my eyes, he never cared about those types of things. Chris was just my bud. We played video games for hours, and he taught me how to skateboard. I taught him how to develop a picture in a darkroom. And then there were those nightly expeditions where we'd lie in the middle of a field and talk about what we thought the future held for us and what part of New York City we'd live in one day. My favorite thing about Chris was his need to look you right in the eye. He felt you couldn't truly connect with someone until you looked him in the eyes.

I cried in his arms over my first broken heart and jumped

Read It?

L. Frank Baum wrote the book *The Wonderful Wizard of Oz* in 1900, and it was so **popular** that Baum wrote about Oz in thirteen more books and three plays.

into them when I got the part of
Dorothy in *The Wizard of Oz*. He
knew all about my life, and I was
always up-to-date on his. My
friends told me that boys and girls
could never be good friends
because the attraction part always
got in the way. I told them they were

For Real?

Cats who are born with
white fur and blue eyes
are more likely to be **deaf**
than cats with other
color eyes.

wrong, that Chris and I were different. He was
like my brother, and I was like his sister. At least, that's how
I viewed our relationship.

Well, apparently this wasn't a two-way street. I found out
one day that Chris viewed our relationship as something
more when he confessed his love to me. Chris's vibrant blue
eyes locked onto mine as I told him that I loved him, yet I
wasn't *in* love with him. At first, he was fine with that decision, and we stayed close friends.

But freshman year slowly crept up on us, and things took
a drastic turn. His soccer buddies began to tease him about
the "girl next door" who had turned him down. Behind my
back, his friends would sit and crack jokes about me, and
soon Chris broke, joining in and slowly picking me apart. The
way I dressed, the way I acted, my personality, my weight and
my skin all became hot targets for teasing. Before I knew it,
the teasing escalated to where there were no boundaries. He
did it to my face.

All of a sudden, I didn't know Chris anymore. He had
morphed into someone else. No more nightly field expeditions, no more CD swapping or sharing secrets. The Chris I
knew was gone. My heart was broken, and my shoulder to cry

on was missing. I started to
question if my friends had
been right in the first place.
Is it possible for guys and
girls to be just friends? My
answer had always been
"yes," but I began to doubt
myself. I began to doubt
everything. Did I ever truly

HOW ABOUT YOU?

Do you think it's **possible** for **boys** and **girls** to be **just friends**?

know Chris? Was the guy I knew and trusted the *real* Chris?

As the months passed, I became more fed up. One day, before class began, I let it all out. I yelled at Chris. I yelled at him for changing and for not being the person I thought he was. For not being my stability when I needed him the most. His response was none other than a blank stare at the floor. I

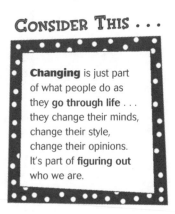

CONSIDER THIS . . .

Changing is just part of what people do as they **go through life** . . . they change their minds, change their style, change their opinions. It's part of **figuring out** who we are.

no longer recognized him. His hair was shaggy, he had gained weight, and he wasn't smiling. He was no longer my best friend.

A whole year later, the Chris I once knew has never fully returned, yet the mean Chris did dissolve. I have come to see that friends fade and people change, as do seasons, but at least you know what season is coming. I thought I knew Chris, and it took me a while to finally realize I didn't. One thing has changed since I came to that realization—he hasn't looked me in the eyes.

Grace French, age 15

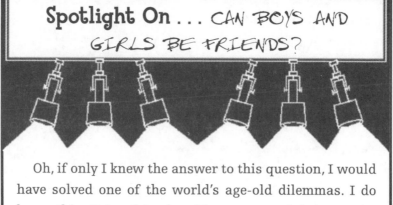

Spotlight On . . . CAN BOYS AND GIRLS BE FRIENDS?

Oh, if only I knew the answer to this question, I would have solved one of the world's age-old dilemmas. I do know this: Being friends with someone of the opposite sex has lots of benefits, like:

- seeing things from an alternative point of view
- having a better understanding of the opposite sex
- less stress than same-sex friendships because competition and jealousy usually isn't an issue
- giving you a chance to do things you might not otherwise try

Now come the possible downsides. Opposite-sex friendships can be confusing because:

- There's always the possibility of attraction.
- Your other friends might not believe you when you say you're "just friends."
- Society tends to assume opposite-sex friends like each other as more than just friends.
- If your friend does crush on you and you don't feel the same, you could lose the friendship.

What do you think are the pros and cons of a boy/girl friendship?

I HAD A FRIEND IN HIGH SCHOOL who had a longstanding crush on me. I knew it. He knew it. In fact, *everyone* knew it. While I liked him as a friend—he was funny, smart and a little goofy—I never had *those* feelings for him. And while I have to admit that I enjoyed the attention he gave me, I never led him on or encouraged him into thinking that he and I had a chance as a couple. I was upfront with him, and I think that's what enabled us to still have a friendship.

But not all such situations always work out as well. Sometimes, after hearing the words "just friends," remaining just that becomes next to impossible, either because the person is embarrassed, too angry or just doesn't know how to handle the situation. The next author has been in the situation of telling a good friend that that's all she wanted from the relationship, and as you can see, it's not always easy, and it doesn't always work out.

CONSIDER THIS . . .

If you watch a Hollywood movie about a **crush**, things always tend to wrap up nicely at the end. The one being crushed on always realizes that her admirer is the real deal, and everyone lives happily ever after. But in **reality**, it **doesn't** always work out that way.

I Called You My Best Friend

I did not know when I took your hand
And held it tight in the dark
That you wanted to hold me forever.
I did not hear your heart breaking
When I told you that I had feelings for your friend.
I am sorry, I really did not know.

I should have opened my eyes
And seen what was seen by you and others.
None of my friends told me.
When my enemies did, I pushed them away,
For I felt they were jealous that I finally found a friend
And that he was popular.

I did not know that your girl-
    friend had broken up with you.
I did not know that your smiles
    were out of the need to hold me
And tell me how you felt.

Did you ever really like me that
    much?
Why would you? I am not the
    prettiest
Or most popular girl in school.
Or was it that you just wanted a girlfriend,
As so many others told me,
As I felt they just wanted to turn me against you.

HOW ABOUT YOU?

Have you ever had a **friend** who started to like you in a **romantic** way? How did you **handle it**?

When I told you the words
I did not know that it was the last time you would speak to me.
I did not know how much you were hurting.
I was in disbelief,
I was flattered.

You left—no good-bye, not even a smile.
When you laughed with the pretty girls,
Was it just to make me jealous?
Congratulations, then, you succeeded.

When I hear your friends talk about you,
I am envious, because you were that good to me—
I just did not see where it was coming from.
I just thought you were a
    sweet guy,
And when I told you my
    secret,
I expected you to keep it.
But you did not.
My words reached
    everybody's ears.
They were meant only for
    you.

Is revenge sweeter now that
    you know that you have
    hurt me?

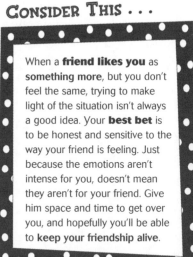

CONSIDER THIS . . .

When a **friend likes you** as **something more**, but you don't feel the same, trying to make light of the situation isn't always a good idea. Your **best bet** is to be honest and sensitive to the way your friend is feeling. Just because the emotions aren't intense for you, doesn't mean they aren't for your friend. Give him space and time to get over you, and hopefully you'll be able to **keep your friendship alive**.

Are you smiling because you won,
And I am the one left with the broken heart, not you?
Are you happy because I am still thinking about you
Even though it happened two years ago?
Or are you missing me,
Thinking about me, wondering what might have been?
Have you ever regretted ignoring me?
Ever thought about giving me a second chance?

They said your feelings were strong.
Were they?
How come you were after her the second I said "no"?
I apologize, again.
I really should have seen it coming.

I would not ask myself these questions
If you had not left me
Alone, to be mocked and gossiped about.
You were part of it, too.
You mocked me and pointed your finger at me,
Through it all.
I thought you were my friend,
My one true friend.

All I can do is apologize and wonder,
If you are laughing with your buddies
Or with your new girlfriend at me,
At my words,
At the truth,
At my stupidity,
At my heart,
At my loss.

I will never know what feelings
    they were,
That took over me
When I thought about you.
Were they of friendship or of something more?

I will never know
What you were to me.
You made me wonder
What my mind was really thinking,
What my heart wanted to say,
When I gave you my hand
And held yours tight.

For Real?

Jealousy is such an **intense emotion** that even the body responds physically. People who experience a jealous streak might feel faint, tremble and start sweating.

Nidhi Chacko, age 15

WHERE DO YOU STAND?

**If a friend crushes on you, and you turn him
down, would you give him a break if he did these things?**

Stopped returning phone calls because it's too painful to hear your voice.

☐ YES   ☐ NO

Asked out your best friend just to make you think he wasn't that into you in the first place?

☐ YES   ☐ NO

Said that your friendship won't change and then started acting completely differently anyway.

☐ YES   ☐ NO

Had trouble looking you in the eye.

☐ YES   ☐ NO

Spread rumors around about you to make you look bad.

☐ YES   ☐ NO

Completely cut you off and pretended you didn't even exist.

☐ YES   ☐ NO

If you said "YES" to more than one of these, then you're definitely a pretty understanding friend. But just because you're understanding doesn't mean that these behaviors are acceptable. If he or she starts acting in a way that makes you feel bad about yourself, that's not okay.

Take the Quiz:

ARE YOU READY TO HANDLE THE BLURRY LINES BETWEEN FRIENDSHIP AND ROMANCE

1. You hoped you were misreading the cues, but it's just been confirmed. Your neighbor and close opposite-sex friend of five years has suddenly developed a huge crush on you. He's following you around like a puppy dog. Unfortunately, you don't share his feelings. What do you do?

   ___ A. You tell your friend how important your relationship is with him, but that you'd rather keep it a friendship because you don't want to risk ruining things. You tell him you'll understand if he needs to not hang around you, but that you hope to stay close friends.

   ___ B. You don't want to break his heart, so you don't give him a definitive answer about your feelings, telling him you need time to think things over. Hopefully, you've just bought a few days to come up with a plan.

   ___ C. You decide to steer clear of him for a while . . . seeing him and talking to him is just too awkward for both of you. You hope he gets over it so you can keep your friendship alive.

2. You're definitely not interested in your friend who has a crush on you, so you can't understand why it bothers you when your BFF confesses to you that she thinks he's hot and is gonna go for it with him. What do you say to her?

   ___ A. You tell her that he's a great guy, and just because it wasn't in the cards for the two of you, maybe they will hit it off and be great together.

   ___ B. You say it's okay with you, but secretly harbor a bit of a grudge. She should know better than to go after this guy. Even if you don't "like" him that way, you can't help but feel an ego boost by his crush on you.

___ C. You ask her how she could go after someone who likes you. Maybe you don't like him back right now, but what if you change your mind down the road?

3. You thought you were getting the same vibe from your close opposite-sex friend, otherwise you never would have told her that you wanted to be "more than friends." You're surprised when she says she doesn't feel the same. How do you handle it?

___ A. You respect her decision and try to keep things in your friendship as normal as possible. Things may not have worked out as you wanted them to, but her friendship is too valuable to risk by being upset.

___ B. You say it's okay, but decide that you'll continue to try to convince her why the two of you would make a great pair by showing her your charming and sensitive side.

___ C. You're hurt that she isn't interested but want to save face with your friends, so you act like it's no big deal and totally shut her out.

4. When you and your close friend realize that you want to take your relationship a step further, you couldn't be more excited. For a while, everything is awesome, and your romance is as tight as your friendship was. But after three months, things start going sour, and you decide to go back to being just friends. What happens next?

___ A. You keep up your end of the bargain, and even though it's a little awkward at first, you decide that with time you'll be able to get your friendship back to where it was.

___ B. You want to make it work, but right now it's feeling too difficult. You let your ex know how you feel, but that you'll continue to care about him or her and hope you can make your friendship work down the road.

___ C. You can't handle the whole friendship thing right now. Every time you see your ex, you get upset at the way things ended, so you back off and close the door on your relationship for good.

5. You thought you could handle it when your ex-boyfriend starts dating your BFF, but suddenly the sight of them walking hand in hand down the hallway sends shivers up your spine. Even though you and your ex have managed to remain friends, you find yourself starting to get upset. What do you do?

___ A. You try to remember why your relationship didn't work in the first place and be happy for the new couple. It clearly wasn't going to work with the two of you, so why bother being so upset?

___ B. You avoid chance encounters with the two of them, figuring if you don't see them together, then how can it bother you? Maybe you'll be able to deal with it eventually, but for now it's best to lay low.

___ C. You know it isn't right, but you put pressure on your friend and your ex to call it off, accusing them of not being considerate of your feelings.

So, how'd you do? Are you ready to handle romance among friends? Give yourself 10 points for every A, 20 points for every B and 30 points for every C. How'd you do?

50–70 points = You're calm, cool and collected about everything having to do with friendships and crushes. You know how to keep your emotions reigned in and value friendship above all else.

80–120 points = Your friendships are important to you, but when love and romance get in the middle, you have a hard time keeping your head on straight. If you're feeling overwhelmed by emotions like jealousy and confusion when it comes to love and friends, get some distance from the situation before taking action.

130–150 points = Yikes! It seems like blurry lines give you some double vision, and you can't see whether you're coming or going when it comes to love and friends. You might want to stick with friendships for now, even when feelings get more intense, because you might not be able to handle the fallout of love gone bad.

CHAPTER 6

WHEN FRIENDSHIPS CHANGE

I t's not inevitable, but it is likely. Even the most rock solid of friendships are bound to change as time goes by—as we change ourselves and as our friends grow in different directions. Change doesn't have to be bad, but it can be hard to go through, especially if your friend is the one changing and you're feeling left behind. This chapter looks at the kinds of changes friendships go through. But fear not—you'll get some tools for dealing with the changes, too.

MY FRIENDS AND I USED TO HAVE what we called the "six-month rule." The six-month rule meant that when a friend had a new boyfriend, she had kind of a "get-out-of-jail-free card" for the next six months. So, if she did insensitive things, like forgetting to return phone calls or neglecting to show up when she was supposed to (generally just not being a good friend), she would be let off the hook. My friends and I knew that when a new love was involved, this behavior was almost inevitable. But after those first six months, things had better get back to normal, whether the relationship was still going on or not. Heads in the clouds cannot last forever.

The first time a friend gets caught up in a new relationship at the expense of other friendships, it's pretty crappy. It's easy to get mad at the friend—until you're in the same position, and you suddenly realize how easy it is to do the exact same thing.

The History of Izzi and Me

I met Isabel on my first day of preschool. I had arrived well-groomed and eager, although a bit nervous about being away from my mother. The first day began with a tour graciously given by one of the teachers. I took note of the festive carpets and a sandbox that looked intriguing. However, what was shown to me last was by far the

For Real?

Many sandboxes are now sand tables. Keeping them raised off the ground helps keeps bugs and other pests out of the sand.

most inviting—a giant trunk of dress-up clothing. As soon as I was left to my own devices, I began digging through the trunk and didn't stop until I had found the prettiest princess costume. I put on the dress and then piled everything else I could find that appealed to me on top. After a half hour and many layers, I was convinced that I looked fabulous.

CONSIDER THIS . . .

Preschool can offer a **strong start** to children's educational lives. Kids who attend preschool:

• have better **social skills**
• have strong **verbal skills**
• have **higher IQs**
• are **more prepared** for elementary school

With the confidence I had gained from my new attire, I worked up the courage to walk over to the pink and blue playhouse in the middle of the room. I stood on the doorstep in my beautiful sparkly dress, poised and ready to make my first real friend. I took a deep breath and knocked on the door. There was no answer, so I waited and knocked again. A few seconds later, a small blonde girl in a pink jumper poked her head through the window, looking around until her eyes settled on me. I looked down at the floor, and then worked up the courage to say, "Hi, my name is Ari. Can I play with you?" She looked at me for a second, thought about it, then abruptly proclaimed "no" and slammed the shutters.

I was devastated and ended up spending most of the day crying and waiting for my mom to come get me. But ever the resilient child, I returned the next day, put on a similar outfit, knocked on the same playhouse door and once again asked to play. The answer was still "no," but I wasn't discouraged. I kept up my efforts until at last I was admitted into the game of house and learned that the girl's name was

CONSIDER THIS . . .

> **Role-playing** (playing house and dress-up) is an **important** part of every **child's development.** Role-playing helps kids become better problem-solvers and learn about social interaction.

Isabel. (I was forced to play the undesirable role of father, but at least I was playing.)

Weeks passed, and I began to play with Isabel every day. I no longer even had to ask. In fact, I had soon secured a monopoly on the role of sister to her role of mother in our epic games of house. Within two months, we had proclaimed each other best friends—we were inseparable.

As soon as preschool ended, we enrolled in a day camp together near her home. After that came ballet classes, swim lessons and gymnastics. Then there were the countless sleepovers. Our mothers even organized a New Year's Eve get-together that quickly became a tradition. I began and ended every year by Isabel's side.

Middle school rolled around, Isabel became "Izzi," and she moved twenty minutes farther away from me. Luckily, Izzi was still the same old Isabel, even with the location change, and we dedicated every weekend to each other. Middle school proved to be difficult, as both of us were put under tremendous pressure, but school was quickly forgotten when I pulled into her driveway for my weekly vacation.

HOW ABOUT YOU?

Every **New Year's Eve**, millions of people make **resolutions** to lose weight, get fit, learn something new or get organized. What New Year's resolutions do you make?

For Real?

The **Power Rangers** were first **popular** in Japan in the mid-1970s before an American TV network executive brought the show over to the U.S.

In eighth grade, I spent New Year's Eve standing in Izzi's backyard watching nearby fireworks and blowing a noisemaker until my face was bright red. By that time, we had spent ten years together, going from loving the Power Rangers and the Spice Girls to going to Weezer concerts together.

That New Year's led me to the year I reluctantly started high school. I had trouble making friends for a while, but I got through it by heading over to Izzi's at every possible occasion. It was a tough year, but eventually we both managed to make groups of friends at our respective schools.

Unfortunately for me, one of Izzi's new friends was an attractive boy with whom she soon became more than friends. Izzi began hanging out with him more and more, and hanging out with me less and less. Soon I was lucky if I got to see her once a month. It got to the point where we would go weeks without talking. Then, one day she called me for the first time in almost a month with shocking news—she and her boyfriend had broken up. She was upset, and while I felt bad for her, I couldn't help but be excited to have my friend back. I rushed over to her house to comfort her and ended up staying for the weekend.

CONSIDER THIS . . .

Do you have a **friend** you've known **forever**? **Long-lasting friendships** have a lot of perks. There's something **comforting** about having friends around who know your history and where you come from.

The next weekend on the way to Izzi's house, everything seemed right with the world. But when I got there, things were different. Instead of running to the door and greeting me, Izzi sat in her room and let her mom answer the door. Izzi didn't get up for a while. I expected that she would be upset about the breakup, but I never realized that it would have impacted her so strongly.

For Real?

Being a teenager can sometimes be like riding an emotional roller coaster. Would it surprise you to know that **7%** of **teens** are **angry** most of the time, and **4%** are **depressed**?

After trying to cheer her up in every way I could think of, I gave up and just asked her what was so special about this guy. She told me that it wasn't the guy that she felt so bad about. What worried her was the way she had handled the whole relationship. Izzi told me that when they started dating, she became so involved that she ignored everything else. She convinced herself that her relationship with this boy was the most important thing in the world, so when it all fell apart she felt like she had lost everything. She felt even worse when she realized that she had sacrificed her relationships with everyone else, especially me. She burst into tears and told me how sorry she was, asking if we could go back to being friends like we had been before she started dating. I told her that, of course, we could.

The next weekend, I went up to her house again. We watched some TV and read magazines, and things felt like they were before. After that, we both made other friends and started dating, but we never went back to ignoring each other like we had before.

This past New Year's Eve, I found myself at Izzi's house again, ringing in the coming year. We blew noisemakers side-by-side, knowing that no matter what happened with college or boys or anything else, we will be able to face it together.

Ariana Briski, age 17

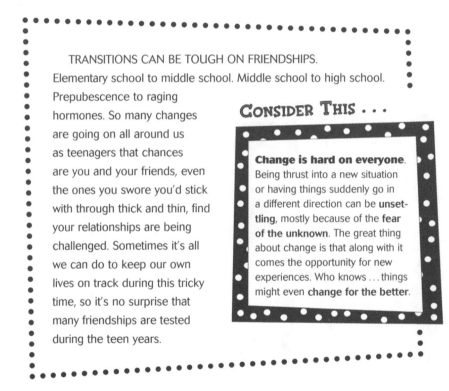

TRANSITIONS CAN BE TOUGH ON FRIENDSHIPS. Elementary school to middle school. Middle school to high school. Prepubescence to raging hormones. So many changes are going on all around us as teenagers that chances are you and your friends, even the ones you swore you'd stick with through thick and thin, find your relationships are being challenged. Sometimes it's all we can do to keep our own lives on track during this tricky time, so it's no surprise that many friendships are tested during the teen years.

CONSIDER THIS . . .

Change is hard on everyone. Being thrust into a new situation or having things suddenly go in a different direction can be **unsettling**, mostly because of the **fear of the unknown**. The great thing about change is that along with it comes the opportunity for new experiences. Who knows . . . things might even **change for the better.**

Friends Forever We'll Always Be

We may not have been the most popular, most loved eighth-graders at our middle school, but we didn't feel the need to be. Becky and I had each other, and we were inseparable. We did all of the same extracurricular activities and never really went anywhere without each other. We were more one person than two separate people. Other kids thought it was annoying that we were so inseparable, but I know that it made me feel more secure and have more confidence. If Becky wasn't there, I wouldn't have made it through school each day, let alone be where I am today.

HOW ABOUT YOU?

Have you ever had a **friendship change** after one or both of you went through a **major life transition**?

Although there were things that made us different—Becky was better at soccer than me, and I was student council president while Becky was just on the committee—we were also the same in many ways. We shared the same name (although she preferred Becky rather than Rebecca), we shared thoughts on many topics, and we shared the same outlook on life. After a while, we rubbed off on each other so much that we ended up sharing our style as well.

CONSIDER THIS . . .

Competition between **close friends** is only **natural** because you're both usually interested in the same things, which is what drew you together in the first place. If the **competition heats up**, try to focus on doing well for yourself as opposed to comparing yourself with anyone else.

By eighth grade we had gone through three years of school together, and we were ready to face high school. We'd heard that many old friends were lost in high school, but Becky and I were *best friends*, and no matter what happened, we knew nothing would tear us apart. We had gone through too many rough times to let what other people said and did bring us down. Friends forever was what we would always be . . . or so we thought.

That summer was awesome. We had a blast spending almost every day together. Although I felt like I was changing on the inside, I knew Becky would be there for me no matter what. We got our schedules when school started

Read It?

In Meg Cabot's *The Princess Diaries*, Mia's friendship with Lilly is put in jeopardy because of the big changes Mia goes through in her training to be the crown princess of Genovia.

and found out that we wouldn't share even one class together that year, but we still felt strong, spending every lunch hour together with our mutual friends and sharing a notebook, which helped keep us in touch with what was going on in our classes and at home.

Then, about halfway through first semester, we started spending less and less time hanging out together. It got to the point where I was listening to other people just to find out what was going on in Becky's life and what she was saying about me. Although we still spent every lunch hour with our mutual group of friends, Becky and I stopped talking. Fewer and fewer pictures of us together appeared in my photo albums. I had to listen to our other friends to find out if she was talking about me, and when they said she was, I believed them without confronting her.

I began to feel lost in our group. Even though I still talked with everyone except Becky, I started spending my lunch hours with new acquaintances. I knew that Becky was changing inside as well. We weren't the inseparable pair anymore—we had become separate people. She played soccer, and I

For Real?

Even though **girls** don't typically play **football**, more and more are playing **rugby**. The sport, which is most popular in Great Britain, Australia and France, is actually the predecessor of football.

played rugby. We saw less and less of each other. As the months went on, I continued to wonder about her and how she had changed. I couldn't believe I had lost touch with my best friend. How could I have let this happen? For some reason, I blamed myself. I broke down many nights just wondering where she was. I missed spending every day with her. I missed our adventures and our sleepovers. I missed just knowing she was there. I missed her family, which I had become a part of.

We started to talk again, but it was actually more like fighting than talking. But then we both got sick of not understanding and blaming each other. We told each other how we really felt. I told her I cried myself to sleep many nights, and she told me she did the same. Although the half-year we spent apart felt like a lifetime, we are slowly making up for it.

Today, we communicate, and we trust each other. That's one thing I will never lose—her trust. I'll never understand why we let something come in and ruin our friendship, why we did the things we did and said the things we said. But we can't go back. High school is tough, but knowing Becky's still in my life and she doesn't hate me is making it easier. I will never forget the good times and bad with Becky, and I'll never lose her trust. I know that from now on, she's not going anywhere.

Rebecca Ruiter, age 15

🌳

OUTSIDE THE BOX

Are you feeling closer to your pet hamster than to your best friend? It's never too late to get your friendship back on track. Try some of these techniques:

- Make a date to have a heart-to-heart with your friend. Make sure he or she knows you want to talk, and pick a place where you won't be distracted by other friends and activities.
- Write a letter to your friend, telling him or her exactly how you feel and how important it is to you that you get your friendship back.
- Don't assume that the friend is trying to blow you off. Consider that he or she might have something going on in his or her life that is distracting or upsetting him or her.
- Don't play the blame game . . . if you really want to repair your relationship, who did or didn't do what isn't the point. Moving forward in a healthy way is.

Spotlight On ... WHEN FRIENDS CHANGE

Do you have a friend who's changing, and it's got you feeling blue? Before you get too down and start to question what's happening, consider this: Everything is constantly changing—leaves fall from trees and grow back again; weather storms come and go; hair keeps growing no matter how many times it's cut; the ocean tide goes in and out. It's just part of nature. Things that spur change in a friend can include:

- moving or switching schools
- something going on in the home, like divorce
- a new interest or hobby

If you see signs that a close friend is changing, follow these three steps before you do anything else:

1. Know that change is normal and doesn't necessarily have to be bad.
2. Unless your friend is changing for the worst and you're concerned about her well-being, give her the space she needs to explore these new interests.
3. Take care of yourself and acknowledge that you are changing even as you read this. Everything we learn, take in and process changes who we are and how we view the world.

I KNOW I'VE BEEN GUILTY OF GIVING too much power to a friend and then feeling helpless and unable to get it back. How about you? Why do we do it? Why do we let someone control the way we're acting and thinking? According to the book *Queen Bees and Wannabes* by Rosalind Wiseman, we give our power to people because they're charismatic. One smile from them can make us feel like a million bucks, so we do whatever it takes to keep those smiles coming.

This next story tells about someone who gave away too much power, but found the strength to claim it back again for herself.

WHERE DO YOU STAND?

Do you ever do things that "aren't you" just because you want to hold on to someone's friendship? Would you . . .

YES NO not try out for cheerleading because your new friends think cheering is lame?

YES NO let a friend continue to cyber bully another kid from your school because you were afraid if you said something you'd be next on her list?

YES NO mouth off to your parents in front of your friends so they'd think you were cool?

YES NO skip out on eating lunch (even if it was your favorite entrée) because all of your friends are dieting and you don't want to stick out?

YES NO accompany your friends on a shoplifting spree because you don't want to seem too straight and say "no"?

Fear or Vertigo

C hildren can be cruel. Teenagers can be cruel. They surround you like hyenas, hunting the weakened prey, slay-
ing them for amusement or, it
seems, merely to fit in.
Entire lives can be destroyed
by this. Entire minds.

"I don't think you were
completely sane that year,"
my best friend Claudia said of
our eighth-grade experience.
That year is a blur to me . . .
a blur of peer pressure and
its consequences, of hidden
messages and terrible guilt. I revisit it in my
nightmares, if only because I'm horrified at my former self, at
this callous thirteen-year-old girl who sought so viciously to
be a member of the pack.

I became close friends with another girl in seventh grade.
In hindsight, I can see that it happened almost too quickly,
too irrationally. By eighth grade, things were starting to cool
down, and I became terrified of losing her friendship. I never
saw her, and when I did, she
rarely spoke to me, as though
I were a piece of furniture in
the background. So I became
desperate to hang on.

Soon I began to take things
she said to me too seriously,

For Real?

Hyenas are sometimes thought
to be **"laughing"** because they
make a strange howling sound
like laughter that can be heard
up to three miles away.
**It lets other hyenas know
they've got food.**

THE WORD

Have you ever experienced **vertigo**?
It's another word for a **dizzy sensation** or the feeling that everything around you is **spinning**.

Seen It?

One of filmmaker Alfred Hitchcock's most famous movies is the thriller *Vertigo* (1958), starring James Stewart and Kim Novak.

and the thoughts that would later make Claudia think me insane began to seep into my mind. For my new friend hated Claudia. With a *passion*. And though I'm not weak, I lacked the bravery to correct my friends. So I sat and silently listened to her go off on Claudia, nodding and hating myself for every minute of it. But I couldn't help it. I was desperate not to lose her friendship. Of course, it's ironic that today I would rather throw myself off a bridge than have her as a friend ever again.

Ninth grade began torturously because I was consumed with self-hatred for what I had done to Claudia (which was basically to humiliate her, torment her and cast her out). I was also angry with

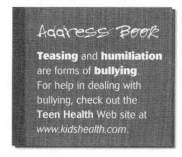

Address Book

Teasing and **humiliation** are forms of **bullying**. For help in dealing with bullying, check out the **Teen Health** Web site at *www.kidshealth.com*.

my new friend, whose halo had faded in the previous year. Suddenly, everything she did infuriated me, probably because somewhere inside I was still hating her for what I had done, for what she had a part in making me do. I began to be bitter, eaten apart inside out, until I couldn't take it anymore. Until I snapped.

I remember when it happened. I was at a party, and I started feeling anxious—my first real panic attack. My mother's family has a history of mental disorders, so I wasn't surprised it was happening, but I was terrified. I felt like the world was crashing down around me, and I wanted to go home where I could be comforted and loved. My friend and carpool mate apparently found my desire to leave the party early unsatisfactory, because she spent the next several weeks mocking me and calling me a hypochondriac behind my back. The mask was off.

THE WORD

A **hypochondriac** is someone who is **convinced** he is sick or about to get sick even when he's perfectly healthy.

I still remember the scent of the garden where I walked outside for an hour at that party. I remember the pounding in my head, the sensation that my life was careening out of control, and there was nothing I could do to stop it. I remember the desperate desire to cry, but the unwillingness to do so. I remember how cool it was that summer night, how scared I was. I remember how confident I was that I would be comforted by my best friend . . . how wrong I was.

At some point that summer, I sat down at my piano and began to pen a song. I don't know where it came from—the lyrics weren't familiar and certainly weren't my style. It was like I was channeling all the anger of my life, all the self-hatred I had struggled with for years, all of those feelings of shock and terror and frustration that the

CONSIDER THIS . . .

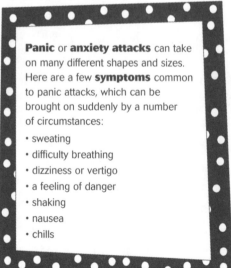

Panic or **anxiety attacks** can take on many different shapes and sizes. Here are a few **symptoms** common to panic attacks, which can be brought on suddenly by a number of circumstances:

• sweating
• difficulty breathing
• dizziness or vertigo
• a feeling of danger
• shaking
• nausea
• chills

one person who should have understood me didn't. My ex-best friend spent three months waging a dirty war against me, and the whole time I didn't say one negative word to her or to anyone else. I kept my mouth closed, except for these lyrics, a burst of self-expression that poured from my lips like molten gold.

HOW ABOUT YOU?

Have you ever **felt** like you were having a **panic** or **anxiety attack**?

> *You thought my life was an open book*
> *But there's so much you didn't know.*
> *You didn't take a closer look*
> *Out of fear, or vertigo.*

There are times when I'm feeling down, and I remember those words. I remember what they meant to me because I had gone from being the terrorist to the victim, and I would be neither from now on. I made a vow never to harm anyone intentionally, never to wage war, never to destroy someone's life as mine had almost been destroyed. And to love forever anyone willing to come into my life. Fear and vertigo no longer exist.

Morgan Halvorsen, age 15

OUTSIDE THE BOX

Journaling can be a great way to get emotions out on paper and keep them from festering inside. Some people find writing song lyrics to be even more freeing. If you're in the mood to jot down some lyrics, here are some tips:

- Write about things that are personal and meaningful to you.
- Listen to music that inspires you while you write.
- Think of lyrics as singable poems.
- Remember that lyrics don't have to rhyme.
- Think about what phrase or phrases might make up the chorus of your song and be repeated.
- Listen to the lyrics of your favorite artists for inspiration and ideas about rhythm, pacing and expression.

IF A FRIENDSHIP DOESN'T LAST FOREVER, does that mean the friendship wasn't real? I don't think so. In fact, I'm a big believer in the notion that some people come into your life when you need them and then fade out of your life when it's time to grow in another direction. And I don't believe that it takes away from how great the friendship was while it lasted.

When I think about friends who have faded out of my life, the one that comes to mind is Wanda. Wanda and I met when I was sixteen, and she was twenty.

Address Book

If you're trying to **track** down a **long lost friend**, a good place to start is the free People Search on Yahoo at *people. yahoo.com.*

We were both working at a summer camp, and after one day of orientation we were joined at the hip. We lived in the same staff cabin, and we spent whatever time we could spazzing out together, listening to music, making jokes and acting like long lost sisters.

When the summer ended, we said our good-byes. I went back to Pennsylvania where I was in high school, and she went back to college in Maryland. We reunited at a camp reunion six months later, but sadly that was the last time we'd see each other. The last I heard from her, she had moved to Florida and was getting married. Now I don't know how to find her anymore since I think she changed her last name.

Seen It?

In the classic movie, *Casablanca* (1942), Ingrid Bergman utters the famous line, "We'll always have Paris."

When I think about the summer that Wanda and I spent together, I can't help but grin, remembering the time we choreographed a dance to a Janet Jackson song and performed it for the rest of the cabin. (Don't all girls do this at some point in their lives?) Wanda was so many things to me that summer . . . a companion, a supporter, a mentor and a friend. And even though we're not in each other's lives anymore, we'll always have our memories of camp.

My Rhiannon

We are galloping. It is a Friday night, and instead of socializing at the movies or shopping at the mall, I am riding horses with my best friend. Bounding over a jump at the same time is our favorite thing. Our time together is virtually untouchable, as if the only world we know is the stretching fields we race in and the beat-up barns where we work and play.

CONSIDER THIS . . .

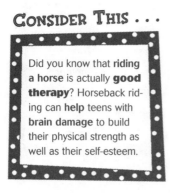

Did you know that **riding a horse** is actually **good therapy**? Horseback riding can **help** teens with **brain damage** to build their physical strength as well as their self-esteem.

She understands me. I know that whether on the back of a horse or walking in a field, we can always talk, and she will keep my secrets. Rhiannon is two years older than me, but our age difference never seems evident when we are together, and neither of us seems to notice or even care.

Rhiannon lives across town, and she goes to a different school than me, so we don't get to see each other as often as we might like. But whenever we can, up to five days a week, we meet out at the farm and catch up on every little detail in the other's life. I ramble on about a new boy in my class, and she explains how one of her good friends is a total flirt and has recently stabbed her in the back for the hundredth time. We share our opinions with each other, and at times even lift the other one up so that we can make it through the hard times.

For Real?
The middle of the sole of a **horse's hoof** is called a **frog!**

Rhiannon was there for my first horse show, never leaving my side. When my horse was difficult, she was there to push me through it, and she helped me keep up my chin when I was so embarrassed that I just wanted to give up. Rhiannon gave me the strength not to.

When it came time for me to leave the farm, we shared a teary good-bye and a long hug. We had promised to keep in touch, to write each other or call, but time passes. Either people forget these things, or we let them lose value more quickly than we should. Both Rhiannon and I were guilty of this.

That was two years ago. Neither of us kept our promise. She would be a sophomore in high school by now, probably walking the halls with

CONSIDER THIS . . .

All **friendships** are **unique**, and even if they don't last forever, they all bring something to your life.

people whose names I am not familiar with. As for me, I have made new friends, too, but every now and then I will run across something that makes me think of her.

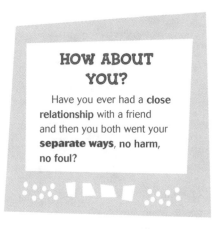

HOW ABOUT YOU?

Have you ever had a **close** **relationship** with a friend and then you both went your **separate ways**, no harm, no foul?

Some people change you. Rhiannon taught me that even when it's hard, sometimes it is okay to move on with life and leave certain people behind, people we may have outgrown or who no longer serve a purpose for us. A part of me sometimes wants to send her a card or pick up the phone and give her a call, but I do not. Instead I just pray that she is doing well and is impacting someone else's life in the way that she did mine.

Kaleigh Vance, age 14

WHAT DO YOU DO WHEN A FRIEND STARTS ACTING IN A WAY THAT CONCERNS YOU? Maybe she starts becoming too obsessed with dieting. Or maybe he starts getting drunk at parties. Or maybe she just plain starts acting like someone you don't know very well at all.

As a teen, I was a late bloomer and very inexperienced when it came to boys. I found safety in my circle of friends, who seemed to feel the same way I did. I knew that no matter what everyone else my age was doing, my friends and I were connected by how we viewed relationships with boys. So when a close friend, one who used to be committed to not going too far with a boy, did exactly that, I didn't know how to handle it.

Read It?

In *Faking 19* by Alyson Noel, Alex starts to feel **pressure** to do things she's **not** cool with just to fit in.

THE WORD

An **intervention** is when one or more people **confront someone** they're concerned about and encourage that person to **seek help**.

I felt hurt. Betrayed. Disappointed. Concerned. But was that just my own baggage? Didn't my friend have a right to make the choices she was making? Was I upset because I was afraid of being left behind by my friends, and that eventually I wouldn't be able to relate to them anymore?

None of these feelings were greater than the concern I felt for my friend. I was at a loss. I knew I was acting differently toward her . . . I've never been good at hiding my feelings. I knew I should have said something, but I also knew that blaming or pointing fingers wasn't going to do any good, and I honestly didn't know how to handle it.

In the next essay, the author does what I couldn't do at the time . . . she approached her friend and shared how she was feeling.

Spotlight On ... WHEN FRIENDS GO IN DIFFERENT DIRECTIONS

When it comes to change, it's not a matter of "if" but "when" and "how." When friends change, it can place a serious burden on the relationship, especially if those changes are for the worse. Smoking, alcohol, drugs, cheating, sex ... all of these can creep into a friendship and split the two of you apart.

If you're the one who isn't changing, and your friend is suddenly no more recognizable than a trick-or-treater on Halloween, the feelings can be pretty intense. You might be feeling:

- down and out
- confused
- isolated and alone
- pressure to change so you don't lose your friend

If you've got a friend or friends who aren't acting like themselves, here are some ways to cope:

- Talk to someone you trust and get some advice on the situation.
- Take the pressure off your relationship by making plans with other friends and exploring other interests.

- Speak up and be honest . . . tell your friend how you're feeling and share your concerns.
- Remember . . . it's not about you. It's about a transition your friend is going through.
- If you don't get anywhere, maybe it's time to reevaluate your friendship and move on.

For Her Own Good

Callie liked Joshua. Really, *really* liked him. She liked him so much that when we all went to camp last summer and she found out that he liked her back, she made some pretty big mistakes with him.

Callie and I have known each other since we were kids. Our moms are best friends. We share the same favorite candy. We used to go to the same school. And even though Callie's younger than me, we tell each other everything. Her relationship is the same with my older sister, Lucy. In fact, we've all been on several vacations together and even used to go rockhounding with our moms! That's hardcore friendship right there.

Seen It?

Camp! (2003) is a comedy musical about a group of teens at a **performing arts** summer camp.

My sister and I were struggling with the things Callie was doing with Joshua when it came to their physical relationship. We knew she was compromising her moral standards, even though in the world's eyes her behavior wasn't abnormal.

Consider This . . .

Most kids go to **summer camp** at some point in their lives. But camping's not just about smores and campfires anymore. Today, you have your **choice** of offerings, including things like:

• Cooking Camp
• Sports Camp
• Robotics Camp
• Circus Camp
• Pottery Camp
• Weight-Loss Camp

We briefly mentioned our concerns to her, but then put it out of our minds.

Then Callie got into trouble with the camp staff for being seen with Joshua after "lights out."

That night, Lucy and I, both counselors at the camp, got permission to sleep with Callie in an empty cabin. We dragged our pillows, sheets and flashlights across the pitch-black campground and proceeded to pull three cots together to make one big bed. Lucy pulled me aside, and we figured out what we would say during "the talk." We decided to be straightforward with her, as we always were, and let her know of our concerns about her relationship with Joshua.

It may seem slightly drastic to abandon our cabins full of little girls and have a makeshift sleepover with a friend who had only been seen hanging out with a boy in the middle of the night. But here's why we did it—she asked us to.

Callie, knowing what she was doing with her boyfriend was wrong, wanted to talk to us. She wanted our help. When a friend is that receptive, you just can't turn her away.

The talk went well, until Lucy and I found out that Callie had been seeing Joshua against her mother's will and that she wasn't planning to stop. We told her she needed to tellher mom about it . . . about *everything*. That got a resounding,

For Real?

One in three **sexually active teens** say they were in a relationship where things "**moved too quickly,**" and nearly one in four say they did things sexually because they felt **pressured** to do it.

"No way! Are you kidding me?!" So, we let it go. After all, we couldn't force her, could we?

As the weeks after camp went by, I talked to Callie several times about Joshua. I found out that she was still seeing him. One conversation revealed even more problems, and my sister and I decided we'd had enough. We stepped up our efforts.

Lucy, the oldest and therefore the one with a more authoritative presence, took Callie out to lunch and told her, "Callie, I love you. You're like a sister to me. That's why I care so much about what you do with Joshua. You know he has detrimental behavior patterns. He has a bad mouth, and he hasn't even been treating you decently. You're being taken advantage of physically, and you don't even seem to care! We've talked with you about it, and it looks like it's not helping. So you're going to have to tell your mom. I know you don't want to, but going behind her back is far worse than the sting of telling her."

When Callie protested, Lucy took a deep breath and said, "Callie . . . if you don't, I will."

I didn't hear much about Callie's reaction other than it wasn't a good one, but I do know this—that day, Callie told her mom about Joshua.

CONSIDER THIS . . .

Getting away for a week or two every summer for **summer camp** has tons of benefits.
You get to . . .
• meet new friends
• be more independent
• discover new talents and interests
• blow off some steam
• try out a new you!

And not just that she was seeing him. She told her that she had compromised her physical standards with him.

Her mom cried with her. Her mom still loved her.

Today, almost a year later, Callie is no longer with Joshua. Today, Callie would tell anyone that she is so glad she broke it off with him. Today, I would tell anyone that I'd go behind my friend's back in a heartbeat just to hear her tell me, like Callie did, "Thank you."

Beth Marshall, age 17

WHERE DO YOU STAND?

Would you speak up and get involved if your friend started acting differently?

You notice her clothes and hair always smell like cigarette smoke.

- I would have to (0 points)
- Depends (1 point)
- Probably not (2 points)

He starts hanging out with a group of football players who are known for taking steroids.

- I would have to (0 points)
- Depends (1 point)
- Probably not (2 points)

You see her downloading a term paper from the Internet to turn in for history class.

- I would have to (0 points)
- Depends (1 point)
- Probably not (2 points)

She goes up to the bedroom with a guy at a party.

- I would have to (0 points)
- Depends (1 point)
- Probably not (2 points)

You catch her in a lie.

- I would have to (0 points)
- Depends (1 point)
- Probably not (2 points)

Add up your points:
0–3 = I need to share my concerns.
4–6 = I'll let some things slide.
7–10 = It's my friend's business, not mine.

OUTSIDE THE BOX

Are you concerned about a friend's behavior? If you want to get involved, it might be time to go to your friend with your concerns. Here are some ideas for a successful intervention with a friend:

- Pick the right time and place to have your powwow. You want to make sure that your friend isn't caught off guard and feels comfortable.
- Start by telling your friend that you're concerned about her and then explain why.
- Choose your words carefully . . . you don't want to put your friend on the defensive. Instead of saying, "You do this and that," try starting with the words, "I feel . . ."
- Have a plan for what you want to say ahead of time so you don't get off track.
- Give your friend a chance to respond to what you're saying.
- Have suggestions for changes you'd like to see in your friend.
- End with a hug and an "I love you!"

CONSIDER THIS . . .

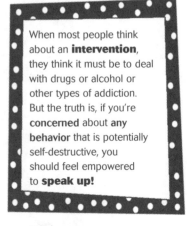

When most people think about an **intervention**, they think it must be to deal with drugs or alcohol or other types of addiction. But the truth is, if you're **concerned** about **any behavior** that is potentially self-destructive, you should feel empowered to **speak up!**

Take the Quiz:
HOW DO YOU DEAL WITH CHANGE IN FRIENDSHIPS

1. You knew things between you and your friend had been strained for a while, but were still thrown off guard when she confronted you and said she thought it was best if the two of you ended your friendship. How do you handle it?

    ___ A. You can't imagine your life without this person in it, so you try to convince her that your friendship is worth holding on to, even though part of you would be relieved to have it over.

    ___ B. You have been feeling for some time that you and your friend were moving in different directions, so you agree it's for the best, tell her you'll always care for her and say *adios*.

    ___ C. You can't believe your friend is doing this to you, and for no real good reason, either. You can't help but get angry with her and try to turn the rest of your friends against her. If she doesn't want you as a friend, then she should lose the rest of the gang, too.

2. You and your circle of friends have always hung out together at parties, but you notice that one of your friends has started sticking with a rougher crowd. Every time you go out, he's been getting out of control. Which reaction is most like something you'd do?

    ___ A. You just don't get why your friend is acting so differently, and it frustrates you to no end. When you run into him at a party, you confront him and ask him what's going on.

    ___ B. You two have never been that close, but you still figure it's worth making sure that you're both really going in different directions before cutting him off completely.

___ C. If he's into partying that much, then maybe he's not the friend for
     you. You figure he's only making himself look bad, and you've got
     plenty of other friends to hang with.

3. **You and a friend from summer camp have known each other
   for years, and even though you don't spend summers together
   anymore, you keep up communication through letters and e-
   mail. Lately, though, she hasn't been in touch, despite your
   attempts to make contact. What do you do?**

___ A. You've been super busy lately, too, and haven't been missing your
     friend that much anyway. You decide that dropping the communi-
     cation would actually be a load off your back, so you let it go.
     Maybe you'll reconnect one day down the road.

___ B. You wonder if you've done something wrong to upset your friend,
     and you step up the communication attempts. You don't want to
     leave this unresolved.

___ C. You do everything you can to get in touch with your estranged
     friend, and when you do, you angrily accuse her of dropping you,
     demanding an explanation.

4. **Your parents invite family friends over for dinner, including
   their daughter who used to be a close friend. In the past few
   years, though, she's been hanging out with a very different
   crowd. How do you handle the dinner party?**

___ A. You protest the whole event, telling your parents that you don't
     want to be stuck hanging out with this girl because you have noth-
     ing in common.

___ B. You embrace your former friend and make the best of the evening.
     You've gone through a lot of changes yourself, but you still have
     the history of your friendship, and that will get you through the
     evening.

___ C. Whether you have a history or not, she's no longer part of your
     crowd, so you treat her like you would at school . . . you ignore
     her.

5. You and your BFF have always been on the same page about just about everything—boys, grades, college—until now. You're not sure what has sparked it, but in the past few months you've noticed your BFF has started behaving in ways that you can't comprehend. What would you be most likely to do?

    ____ A. While you love your friend, you also know that you can't control her and the decisions she makes. You are honest with her about the way you're feeling and share any concerns with her, but realize that maybe the two of you are just drifting apart.

    ____ B. The fact that this person whom you once trusted with your darkest, deepest secrets is now acting like someone she's not is very unsettling to you. What about all the promises you made to each other about being friends forever? Not knowing what else to do, you cut off all communication with her.

    ____ C. You're upset about changes in your friend, and at the earliest chance possible decide to try to fix things. The two of you vowed to stick together, and she's not keeping up her end of the bargain.

So, are you cool with it when friendships change? Give yourself the following points:

1. a = 20, b = 10, c = 30; 2. a = 30, b = 20, c = 10; 3. a = 10, b = 20, c = 30; 4. a = 20, b = 10, c = 30; 5. a = 10, b = 30, c = 20.

50–70 points = You know that life is always changing, and we're all constantly growing and moving in different directions. You accept that you can't control anyone else, only the way you feel. Your ability to accept change doesn't mean that you won't intervene if you have concerns; it just means that you know how to let things go when they are out of your hands.

80–120 points = Change seems to throw you for a loop, especially when it concerns your friends. If you had your druthers, you and your best friends would be sitting around telling stories about the good old days fifty years from now, and you'd still be just as close.

130–150 points = You're a creature of habit, and any change, especially when it involves your nearest and dearest, is seen as a threat to your very being. Try to remember that other people's changes usually don't have anything to do with you . . . there's no need to take it personally.

CHAPTER 7

TOUGH STUFF

Friendships can be painful, especially when tragedy strikes and someone we love is suddenly taken away from us. This chapter deals with the grief of losing a friend.

HAVE YOU BEEN IN AN ACCIDENT OR HURT YOURSELF WHILE PLAYING A SPORT OR FOOLING AROUND? I broke my ankle playing tennis once. One second I was a Vanessa Williams wannabe running around on the court, and the next I looked like Jim Carrey taking a pratfall. In lunging for a ball, I stepped on it instead. Doh! I knew my ankle was broken . . . not to be graphic, but I heard it snap. And as I lay there on the court, I just wanted to kick myself (with the foot that wasn't hurt, of course).

How am I going to run the Race for the Cure in a few weeks? How am I going to get around my three-story apartment on crutches? How will I get to work on the subway in a cast? When will it stop hurting? Questions filled my brain, but the loudest one screaming inside my head was: *Why did this have to happen to me?* More than anything, I wanted that moment back, to rewind the past five minutes and do it all again, this time being careful not to step on the yellow orb bouncing in front of me.

If you've experienced a moment when you wish you could just turn back time and make different choices, you know that the desire can be really strong, especially when the moment involves an accident that is life-altering.

The Little Red Bunny

Even though I haven't lived my entire life yet, I know that I will never have a worse day than January 4, 2002.

It was a frosty Saturday morning, and we woke up to the sweet smell of pancakes and fried bacon. My friend Justine and I jumped out of bed at the sound of plates clattering and skipped down the stairs of her cabin in McGregor, Minnesota. We had just finished our huge break-fast when we decided it was too nice to stay inside. So we got bundled up and went out.

For Real?

Four-wheelers are also known as **ATVs** (all-terrain vehicles). Most states have age restrictions, making it illegal for young teens to operate them. The U.S. Consumer Product Safety Commission is trying to **ban** the use of ATVs by anyone under sixteen because they are so **dangerous**.

"I wanna go four-wheel-ing so badly!" moaned Justine, knowing her dad would never let her drive. "Let's go ask Krissy and see if Dad will let her drive us!"

"Sweet! Let's go!" I said, not knowing my life was about to horribly change.

Krissy, Justine's cousin, only fourteen at the time, was allowed to drive the four-wheeler, so we decided to go for a quick ride on the trails. I was on the back with Justine in the middle. Being on the back was scary. It was almost like I knew something bad was about to happen. I had butterflies dancing in my stomach.

"We should go on the North Road!" Krissy yelled over the roaring engine.

Without reply, Krissy sped out of the forest trails and stopped on the side of the road. I was looking at Justine. She was so happy, so full of life. She was laughing the whole time.

"Yeah, we should!" Justine replied happily.

Krissy looked both ways for cars and then hit the gas. The road was half gravel and half ice, and it scared me because I knew we were going very fast. But when I heard Justine's laughter over the screaming engine, I started to feel better.

If she isn't scared, then why am I? I asked myself.

When we got to the end of the road, we made a loop around and went again. I was just starting to have fun when we hit an icy patch. Krissy lost control near a ditch, and the whole four-wheeler fell over with Krissy, Justine and me on it!

HOW ABOUT YOU?

Have **you** ever been **scared** about something, but **not spoken up?**

When I woke up, I was lying in the middle of the road. My head was throbbing, but I got up fast and tried not to cry at the excruciating pain to show the girls I wasn't a baby. It felt like I had been stabbed in the head a thousand times. I couldn't even see straight. I had to cry. But before I could, I saw Krissy. She was standing there, looking at the ground in horror. So I looked down. The sight of my best friend lying there helplessly sent chills through my body. I just stood there staring at the body of my friend who had once been so full of life. I was in total shock. I couldn't move. I couldn't breathe. All I could do was stare. It felt like I was having a nightmare until I started to cry, but not because of the pain in my head. Krissy was crying, too.

A car drove up, and I saw that it was Justine's dad. Soon her cousin drove up on another four-wheeler. An ambulance drove up, then another. Krissy and I just stood

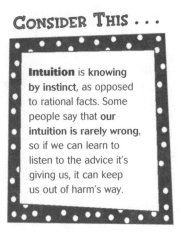

CONSIDER THIS . . .

Intuition is knowing by **instinct**, as opposed to rational facts. Some people say that **our intuition is rarely wrong,** so if we can learn to listen to the advice it's giving us, it can keep us out of harm's way.

For Real?

Teens and children account for **40%** of **injuries** and **deaths** in ATV accidents— more than 60,000 a year.

there, sobbing and holding each other. Everyone was huddled over my best friend, but Krissy and I started to walk back to the cabin.

"I'm so sorry," Krissy said between sobs.

As she said that, we could feel the cool breeze from the helicopter overhead. I could tell that Krissy knew something I didn't.

Death hadn't even crossed my mind. I pictured Justine in a hospital, never a coffin.

Krissy and I sat on the couch staring blankly at each other, not saying a word. But we both knew what we were thinking. We were waiting to hear the news from Justine's father when her aunt came back crying and made me put ice on my head. That was the last thing I cared about.

The ambulance came and took us away. The medics asked if I was okay, but I was still in complete shock. I couldn't cry. As much as I tried to tell myself what had happened was real, I couldn't be convinced. I never thought this would happen to me. I just wanted to go home and forget about the whole day.

When we arrived at the hospital, they did a bunch of tests on Krissy and me. I was lying in the bed all alone, and a nurse came over with

CONSIDER THIS . . .

Being involved in a **traumatic accident** can send your body into **shock**. Symptoms of shock include:

- cold and clammy skin
- sweating
- fast or slow pulse
- irregular breathing or hyperventilating
- confusion

WHERE DO YOU STAND?

Trusting your instincts can help you stay out of a tough spot. What would your instincts tell you about these situations?

A friend repeatedly shows up to school with bruises, and he always has a different excuse for how they got there.

- Something's not right   (1 point)
- Nothing to worry about   (2 points)

Your friend wants the two of you to get a ride home from a party with an older student. He says he hasn't been drinking but is acting a little odd.

- Something's not right   (1 point)
- Nothing to worry about   (2 points)

You notice that your BFF suddenly starts dodging to the bathroom after every meal.

- Something's not right   (1 point)
- Nothing to worry about   (2 points)

You jump on the Internet in the library and find that the last person using it was checking out sites about weapons.

- Something's not right   (1 point)
- Nothing to worry about   (2 points)

You notice some of the star baseball players in the locker room are taking pills they say are aspirin, but they act kind of nervous when they see you.

- Something's not right   (1 point)
- Nothing to worry about   (2 points)

Add up your points:
5–7 = You're tuned in!
8–10 = You're a little out of touch.

a stuffed, little red bunny. She said that a church had donated it and I could have it. I waited forever for my parents to arrive. When they came, they were both crying. They hugged and kissed me until I felt smothered. We drove home in silence. I couldn't sleep.

I didn't cry until I went to the funeral and then it hit me . . . hard. I saw Justine's whole family there and all of my friends from school. Almost our entire grade skipped school to go to her funeral.

After that, school just didn't feel the same for me. My friends acted like the whole thing hadn't happened. But my whole life changed. I get headaches and heartaches a lot easier. I will never forget my best friend. And as much as I wish I could, I'll never forget that horrible day. But I will always treasure the little red bunny that comforted me when I needed it most.

Anne Braten, age 14

Spotlight On . . .
MAKING SENSE OF TRAGEDY

When tragedy strikes, it can be difficult to come to terms, let alone make any sense of it. Our bodies and brains go into an emotional shock, as if they don't know how to deal with the news. It's completely normal to feel emotions like fear, confusion, anger, sadness, frustration, emptiness . . . even hopelessness. The hardest part about accidents and tragedies is that there is usually no rhyme or reason as to why it happened in the first place. We're left wondering how life can be so random, so out of control. And while it's true that sometimes tragedy changes us and who we are, we all have the ability to get through it with the right support.

They say that time heals all wounds, but that's not necessarily true. While time does help you get distance from the tragedy, unless you spend that time trying to deal and cope with what's going on, you might not get over it emotionally. Here are some things you can do to help with the healing process when dealing with a tragedy in your life:

- Talk about it as much as you can and with people who really know how to listen.
- Don't hold in your feelings. Express them however you know how—crying, playing guitar, shouting, exercising, talking. If you keep your feelings inside, you'll eventually have to find a way to get them out, and you might not do it in the healthiest of ways.
- Surround yourself with supportive and loving people. Right now you need the hugs, pats and love of people who want to see you happy.
- Don't feel bad if you catch yourself smiling or having fun. Feeling happiness doesn't mean that you are forgetting the victims of tragedy.
- Keep doing things that you love and keep up your routines. The more you can spend time doing your "normal" things, the more normal you will feel.
- Be patient. Give yourself time to get over the tragedy, and don't feel that you have to get over it as quickly as someone else. We all handle tragedy differently.

I SPENT MANY OF MY TEENAGE YEARS waiting for the other shoe to drop. I just had this feeling that life was tough (which it is) and that bad things would happen to me and those around me (which they sometimes do). The problem is, it was getting me pretty down. In fact, I started spending so much time worrying about what *might* happen that I forgot to enjoy what actually *was* happening.

I eventually put it together that while I couldn't change the future, I could change how I felt in the meantime. The choice was mine: worry about the future constantly and not enjoy the present, or live in the present and deal with the future when it happens. I decided to live in the present, and after going through a tragedy, so did the author of this next story.

My Loss

Most of us live under the false perception that everyone we know is immune to bad things happening. We see friends and family members as individuals who are so untouched that unfortunate events and catastrophes never dare to prod their everyday living. The media is full of war news, death tolls and freak accidents, but as a nation we merely shake our heads, feel quick sympathy, perhaps donate some money to charity from time to time, then come back to our reality, treating life, ourselves, *our loved ones*

CONSIDER THIS . . .

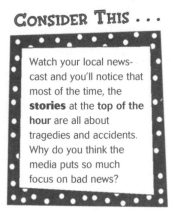

Watch your local news-cast and you'll notice that most of the time, the **stories** at the **top of the hour** are all about tragedies and accidents. Why do you think the media puts so much focus on bad news?

Seen It?

Michael Moore's Academy Award–winning documentary, *Bowling for Columbine* (2002), takes a look at how the media thrives on tragedy.

like infinite people we'll never see encased in a coffin.

My earth-grounding reality check arrived in the appearance of Victoria, a girl with a charming smile, great hair and a booming, adrenaline-pumped personality. I met her sophomore year when I was still trying to adjust to the high-school world. At the time, everyone was going crazy due to the immense workload and cranky teachers pushing us to know the difference between a parabola and a hyperbola.

For some reason, my name was notorious in all of Mr. Farley's English classes. He loved to bring it up because it was unique, and my notes were, in his words, "extraordinarily specific." This is how Victoria heard my name for the first time.

"Ohhhh . . . so you're Lovely!" she exclaimed with delight when another friend introduced us. "Crazy . . . Farley mentions you, like, every day in our class."

"Right . . ." I said uncomfortably, shifting my weight to my other foot, embarrassed that someone knew me through my nerdiness instead of my coolness. "Nice to meet you. Hopefully we can hang out sometime."

And we did. Days later, Victoria knew me not only for my geeky qualities, but also for my love of clothes, my inability to cook and the fact that I write from the heart. We grew closer each day, laughing about things only fifteen-year-olds would understand, braiding hair into cornrows every week to stand

Read It?

The new book *Teens Cook: How to Cook What You Want to Eat* by Megan Carle helps teens who are **afraid** of the **kitchen** to get cooking!

apart from the crowd and hugging each other like sisters. Yet
all this changed when she decided to switch tracks to pursue
her dreams of being a musician. I was definitely distraught,
but she reassured me that we would never sever our bond,
that we'd see each other in school every two months. So she
left with the promise that we were friends deep within our
souls, and our relationship could
never be tested.

Months passed, and I bloomed into
a junior, now sixteen years old and
not as lame as before, with a handful
of friends and a high GPA to boot. As
time slipped away, I forgot Victoria
and our friendship—forgetting her
existence, forgetting her smile, forgetting her soul. The promise of our

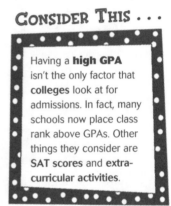

CONSIDER THIS . . .

Having a **high GPA**
isn't the only factor that
colleges look at for
admissions. In fact, many
schools now place class
rank above GPAs. Other
things they consider are
SAT scores and **extracurricular activities**.

endless companionship quickly deteriorated, and I grew
indifferent toward her. When I saw her walking in the halls,
I'd stride by with an unexplainable bitterness coursing
through my veins, believing that she had changed for the
worse, that she felt that she was above my level.

The one time I attempted to start a conversation by asking
her how she was doing, a mere three words were the only
response to my effort before she walked on without even
looking back. "Oh, I'm fine," she said simply.

Sometimes I found myself looking at her from a distance
when she was alone. I knew that she was looking at me, too,
but I blatantly ignored her friendly gestures to inflict the
hate back, to be cold and detached, to signify that I'd forgotten her. She was stuffed into the corner of my mind with dust

CONSIDER THIS . . .

> Hate is an intense emotion, and the word **hate** shouldn't be thrown around carelessly. The next time you're about to say that you hate someone, try replacing the word with **"strongly dislike."** The emotions that go along with it aren't as intense, or as destructive.

bunnies and worries. I took her for granted, and now I wish I hadn't, that I would've taken the chance to talk to her when she was alive.

In June 2004, Victoria got into a car accident on the California 2 Freeway. The car flipped several times and was totaled when it hit the ground. She was on her way to lunch with a bunch of friends she had met a week before, novice drivers who were confident enough to tackle the freeway. She wasn't wearing a seat belt, and she suffered severe head trauma and slipped into a coma. She died a few days later.

When I learned the news, my body went numb, and I just sat there with eyes wide open, spitting the words, "Oh, my God" twenty times over. During the funeral, I held my friend's hand and stared ahead at Victoria's sobbing sister, the mournful priest and her glistening white coffin. I felt ashamed when tears rolled down my cheeks, a sudden disgrace for crying over a person I had purposely forgotten, a friend who passed away not knowing how much her short companionship meant to me. I felt I had no right to cry, no right to visit, for she would never understand why I was there in the first place when I had condemned her as a forgotten friend.

For Real?

Car accidents are the leading **cause of death** for teenagers, mostly due to factors like lack of experience, not wearing seatbelts, tailgating, alcohol and drowsiness.

Right after the Mass, I had to go back to the real world, ironically stopping by the DMV office for my sister to take her driving test, seeing teenagers pass by so joyous for their permit, while I, dressed in black, fought with my sadness, clutching in my hand a prayer given for her during the wake.

Nothing lasts forever. We hear this all the time in Hollywood movies and tragic stories in the news, yet so often we turn our backs from this message like it doesn't apply to our own lives. But look closely and you'll see the world turning in constant turbulence, never stopping for you or your loved ones to glide through life forever. At some point in our lifetimes, we will all experience tragedies, so don't wait until it's too late. We are finite—it's better to love and appreciate now.

Read It?

Robert Frost's famous poem, *Nothing Gold Can Stay,* talks about **appreciating** what we have in the **present** because **nothing lasts forever**.

Lovely Umayam, age 17

OUTSIDE THE BOX

There are some people who go through life yearning to be somewhere else. When I was ten years old, I wanted to be sixteen. By the time I hit sixteen, I just wanted to be twenty-one. When I hit thirty, I wanted to be twenty-five. Why are we never content with where we are today and instead always looking to be something, or somewhere, else? Maybe it's because we haven't mastered the art of "living in the moment." When people live in the moment, they fully appreciate where they are and what they're doing at the moment they're doing it.

If you want to make an effort to live in the moment, here are some tips:

- When you are having a conversation with someone, really listen to what they're saying and avoid the temptation to only half-listen because you're too busy figuring out how you're going to respond.
- Tune into your body. A good time to do this is when you're lying in bed. Go through your body from your head to your toes and focus on different areas as you totally relax, feeling where you hold tension and getting more in touch.
- When you're doing something and feel a sense of happiness, try to take notice that you're feeling happy and enjoy it! Don't worry about what will happen later that day or when the moment ends.
- Spend a few minutes every day just being silent . . . lying with your eyes closed in bed or maybe sitting outside in the backyard listening to the birds and smelling the flowers.

ONE OF THE MOST DIFFICULT LESSONS I'VE LEARNED IN MY LIFE is that I can't control other people. No matter how much I love or care for someone, at the end of the day they're going to make decisions on their own, and I can't blame myself if they make bad choices.

THE WORD

Regret means to remember with a **feeling** of **sorrow**.

Perhaps this lesson is never more clear than when we lose someone to suicide. Statistics show that suicide is the third most common cause of death among teens and young adults. Chances are, we've all known someone who's killed himself, and if you have, you know that suicide is incredibly painful for everyone involved. The people who are left behind, especially close friends and family, find themselves lost and wondering *why?* Guilt is overwhelming. *What could I have said that would have made a difference? Didn't he know I loved him? Didn't she realize that life wouldn't be the same without her?*

Finding peace of mind when dealing with the suicide of a friend or loved one can be difficult. These next two authors explore their feelings of loss in the form of poems.

Regret

I regretted the decision for days at a
time.
Wishing I had done something that
would have changed her mind.
It was obvious she was unhappy, and
even though the choice was hers,

CONSIDER THIS . . .

Some people believe that feeling **regret** is a **waste of time** because we can't change the past. Do you agree with this?

I wondered if I could have
stopped her, or was her
life just all a blur?

I question what would
cause someone to want
to take her life,
To end it right then and
there, without putting
up a fight.
I try to put myself in her
position at the time,
And wonder what she was
thinking, what was
going through her
mind?

Someone please assure
me I had done all that
I could.
Assure me there was
nothing I could've
done that would have
changed the way she
was.
I think of her every day,
missing her to death.
Convincing myself she's
all right now, and that
this was just a test.

Alex Zuber, age 14

WHERE DO YOU STAND?

How do you handle it when your emotions get involved?

When I'm mad, I . . .

A. find a healthy way to get it out
B. get advice on how to handle my anger
C. keep it bottled up inside

When I'm overwhelmed, I . . .

A. take a deep breath
B. look for help
C. pretend everything's okay

When I feel concern, I . . .

A. figure out what's going on
B. share it with others
C. brush it off

When I'm scared, I . . .

A. face my fear head-on
B. look for support
C. act like everything's fine

When I'm sad, I . . .

A. cry and get it out
B. find a shoulder to lean on
C. try to be tough

How did you do?

Mostly As = I express my emotions and resolve things head-on.

Mostly Bs = I acknowledge when I need help, and I know where to get it.

Mostly Cs = I don't know a good way to express my emotions.

Why Didn't You Try?

They say that you were depressed
And that you had been for a while
They say that you weren't happy
That you couldn't take it anymore

But you were only sixteen
And way too young to die
You had your whole life ahead of you
So, why didn't you try?

They say that you felt all alone
And as if no one cared
But don't you know you weren't alone
For I was always there

They say that you put on a smile
To put everyone at ease
But at night when you were all alone
You'd cry yourself to sleep

But you were only sixteen
And way too young to die
You had your whole life ahead
    of you
So, why didn't you try?

After a while you decided to give up
You didn't think life was worth the pain
So you climbed the stairs two at a time
Went to your room and ended it all

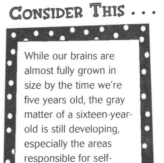

CONSIDER THIS . . .

While our brains are almost fully grown in size by the time we're five years old, the gray matter of a sixteen-year-old is still developing, especially the areas responsible for self-control and judgment.

Address Book

If you're feeling **suicidal**, people are on hand to **help** you right now. Try calling one of these **hotlines**:
• Suicide & Crisis Hotline has a toll-free number (1-800-999-9999)
• Hopeline (www.hopeline.com) has a toll-free number (1-800-SUICIDE)

I was at camp enjoying myself
When I got the call from Mom
I completely lost it and fell apart
I hadn't even known something
    was wrong

So now I sit here all alone
And think of all I've lost
You took your life and left me
    here alone
Now all I can do is cry

But you were only sixteen
And way too young to die
You could have had an amazing life
If you had only tried.

For Real?
One in every twenty
teenagers is **depressed**.
Studies show that **girls**
are **more than twice**
as likely to be
depressed as boys.

Mandy Pike, age 18

HOW ABOUT YOU?

Have you ever **known**
someone who's committed
suicide or attempted to?
How did it make **you feel**?

OUTSIDE THE BOX

When someone we know commits suicide, it leaves us feeling all kinds of emotions: guilt, frustration, sadness, confusion. The biggest thing we struggle with is wondering if we could have done something to prevent it from happening. If you're struggling to deal with the aftermath of a friend's suicide, here are some ideas for helping you get through it:

- Talk to someone about how you're feeling . . . while it's okay to feel sad and regret the loss of your friend, harboring guilt will only prolong your healing process.
- Write a letter to your friend, saying everything you would say to her were she still alive. Getting your thoughts out will be therapeutic.
- Keep your friend alive in your memories. Just because a person isn't here in the flesh doesn't mean that we can't still celebrate him and his life. By remembering the good times and happy memories, we can keep that part of him alive.
- Get involved in a suicide survivor group to get the support you need. You can find information on support groups near you at the Survivors of Suicide Web site: www.survivorsofsuicide.com.

NO MATTER WHAT YOU BELIEVE ABOUT LIFE AFTER DEATH, there's no doubt that people who've passed on continue to live in some way on Earth. How? We keep them alive. Every time we look at a picture or reread a letter or think about a memory that involves these people, we are keeping them and their energy in the present.

My granddad used to bite my cheeks when I was a kid. You have to understand that I have very malleable, fun-to-bite cheeks (or so I've been told). Anyway, when he'd bite me, I'd scream and squeal, both from pain and from delight. And even though I pretended to hate it, I loved it because I knew he did it because he loved me, big cheeks and all. And now as I think about that memory, I can still get that feeling back, that feeling of joy and happiness, even though my granddad passed away a long time ago. If someone touches you in your life, the power of memory alone will keep him alive.

Jerry

Back in early fall 2000, I met a person who would change my life forever—my friend, my brother, Jerry. Jerry was different from other kids. He had been born with such severe health and mental problems that his mother and family couldn't take care of him, and he was placed in foster care.

Read It?

I Will Remember You by Laura Dower is a guidebook aimed at helping teens **deal with the grief** of death.

When I met Jerry at a residential treatment facility in Pittsburgh, he was thirteen years old and only four feet seven inches tall. He had very short black hair and big brown eyes. I

THE WORD

Sleep apnea is a condition where the brain forgets to tell the body to **breathe** when it's asleep. People with sleep apnea sometimes sleep with an oxygen mask.

loved him immediately. For the next month or two, we visited him in Pittsburgh, and he came to our home to visit us. During his short visits with us, Jerry and I talked, went to the store and watched TV. Jerry became one of my foster brothers four days before Christmas 2000.

Over the next two years, the bond between Jerry and I grew. He became more than a friend to me—I thought of him as a brother. Despite Jerry's physical limitations, we would play Wiffle Ball and go swimming. We would go camping with the family. At night, Jerry needed to be hooked up to oxygen to help him breathe, and a machine monitored his pulse. If he stopped breathing, an alarm would go off and wake us so we could help him.

Mom showed me how to hook up Jerry to the machines, and every night at bedtime, Jerry would hop on my back and I'd carry him downstairs to his room. The machines were noisy, and my room was right next to his, but I didn't mind. Jerry would yell "goodnight" to me, and I would yell "goodnight" back. I lay in bed and listened to his machines until I fell asleep.

Jerry had a reputation for being a troublemaker, but I loved him anyway. Eventually, he

For Real?

The most common way that **kids** in **foster care** exhibit **mental-health problems** is through bad behavior, like being overly aggressive or trying to get attention in not-so-great ways.

was placed back in and out of institutions and group homes because of his behavior. I continued to visit him in these institutions all over Pennsylvania. At some point, Jerry ran out of institutions in Pennsylvania due to the extreme level of care he required, so he went to a home in Oklahoma. Before he left, he was allowed a short home visit with us. I saw him for only two hours. That was the last time I would see Jerry, even though I talked to him on the phone every now and then and told him that I loved him.

On June 1, 2003, we received a call from the group home in Oklahoma saying that Jerry had died. I completely broke down. I didn't know what to say. I couldn't breathe. It felt like the walls were closing in on me. We went to Jerry's hometown for the viewing and funeral. We finally got to meet Jerry's real family—his mom, brother, sister, cousins, grandparents and nieces. At the viewing, his family had made a collage that included pictures of all of us, and we all had a chance to say one last good-bye to my friend, my brother, Jerry. Even though he's gone, I'll always love him . . . just like a brother.

Andrew Woods, age 17

Take the Quiz:

DO YOU KNOW HOW TO HANDLE
TOUGH STUFF WITH YOUR FRIENDS ?

1. You and your friend just had a big blowup on the phone, and you're absolutely furious. You can't believe your friend said such hurtful things to you. What do you do?

   ___ A. You go to your room, slam the door and start throwing stuff around. When you're this angry, you tend to get out of control, and there's no calming you down.

   ___ B. You go for a walk to get some fresh air and chill out for a while. Once you and your friend have both cooled off, you'll try to set things straight.

   ___ C. You are completely annoyed, but feel like the situation is hopeless. You decide to give your friend the cold shoulder until he apologizes to you.

2. You know your friend is a cutter, but suddenly her cuts are looking deeper and more serious. You're especially alarmed because your friend has been acting obsessed with suicide and talking about what happens after death. What's your approach?

   ___ A. You know that this is one problem that's way over your head. You go to your mom and let her know about your concerns. Together, the two of you come up with a plan of action.

   ___ B. You're conflicted between being worried about your friend and not wanting to get her into trouble. You're afraid of upsetting her by bringing attention to her cutting, so you decide to just keep a closer eye on her instead.

___ C. You decide to do some online research and try to find some resources that will help you know what to say when you talk to your friend. You don't want to betray her confidence, but you can't let this slide either.

3. You and a friend are involved in a serious car accident as your friend's mom was driving you to the movies. You walked away with only a few bruises, but your friend is in critical condition and fighting for her life. You know the accident wasn't your fault, but you can't help but wonder why you are fine and she's so hurt. How do you handle the guilt you're feeling?

___ A. You put on a happy face when you're around your friend's family. They have enough to worry about without worrying about you, too. Besides, you're fine, physically.

___ B. You are overwhelmed with guilt and confusion, and find yourself feeling despair about the future. You feel like you're spiraling out of control, but decide to try to handle it on your own.

___ C. You know that the way you're feeling isn't healthy, nor is it going to get better unless you deal with the emotions involved. You confide in a close friend and ask for help.

4. You arrive at school Monday morning to find the hallway abuzz with the news that a kid in your grade died of alcohol poisoning Saturday night. You weren't close friends with the boy, but you have known him since second grade, and you find yourself shaken by the news. What would you do?

___ A. Even though you weren't close friends with the boy, you're feeling genuinely upset, and you're not afraid to show it. You take advantage of the grief counselors brought in by the school to find tools for dealing with your feelings of loss.

___ B. You and the boy weren't good friends, so you feel like it's not your place to act all upset about it. You're pretty freaked out, but you decide to play it cool. No one would understand why you were upset anyway.

___ C. You mourn the loss of the boy without making a big deal about it. You're a little embarrassed by your emotional response, so you stay home sick a couple of days to get over it.

5. One of the guys in your group of friends has been sending out signals that he wants to settle a score with another kid in school. You know his father has guns lying around the house, and your friend has made it no secret that he would love to use one. What do you do?

___ A. You can't deal with your friend's issues right now, so you just ignore him when he makes threats and talks about weapons and ammo. He's an all-talk-no-action kind of guy anyway, so there's probably nothing to worry about.

___ B. You find it hard to believe that your friend is serious about doing something violent, but you decide to keep a closer eye on the situation anyway. If you see any more signs that he is about to do something violent, you'll stop him from doing it.

___ C. You are worried that your friend might do something stupid and hurt someone else and maybe himself, as well as jeopardize his entire future. You confide in a teacher or guidance counselor you trust so that the appropriate action can be taken.

So, what's your approach when things get tough? Give yourself the following points:

1. a = 10, b = 30, c = 20; 2. a = 30, b = 10, c = 20; 3. a = 20, b = 10, c = 30; 4. a = 30, b = 10, c = 20; 5. a = 10, b = 20, c = 30.

50–70 points = High drama has never been your thing, and you try to avoid getting involved in anything dramatic at all times. You figure that the easiest way to deal with difficult situations is to pretend they don't exist and maybe they'll go away.

80–120 points = You spend a lot of time debating plans of action in your head because you want to do the right thing, but you don't always know how you should be feeling or what action you should take.

130–150 points = You're clearly the person to turn to in a crisis. You don't lose your head when things get difficult, and you're usually able to think clearly and take steps to make sure a bad situation doesn't get worse. In fact, with your help, things could get much better in a hurry.

CHAPTER 8

FRIENDS IN NEED

Perhaps nothing rocks our world more than when a friend is going through a rough time. Whether it's problems at home or a friend who gets sick or hurt, we never feel more helpless than when we're watching a friend in need. This chapter looks at the powerful ways friends can lean on each other when they need help the most, and gives some ideas for helping a friend going through a rough time.

WHEN A FRIEND LEAVES—BY MOVING OUT OF TOWN, by becoming a different person and drifting away, or as the result of a painful breakup—it's never easy. Even in friendships that were unhealthy to start with, a friend's absence can feel lonely. Some people would rather have not-so-good friends than no friends at all, and others hold on to relationships that are destructive, unhealthy or just plain not fun because they figure it's better than sitting home alone on a Friday night with nothing to do but stare at your IM Buddy List when not even one person is online.

But who says that these are the only two choices: not-so-great friends on the one hand or no friends at all? In fact, what if a new friend with great potential, one who shares your thoughts, dreams, even your sense of humor, is waiting right around the corner? And what if this phenomenal friendship never has the chance to happen because you're too wrapped up in one that's not so satisfying?

They say that losing one friendship can open up the door for new ones. Well, as you'll read in this next story, it can reopen the door to old friendships, too.

CONSIDER THIS . . .

What's your **definition** of a **friend?** If you know what you look for in a friend, then you'll accept nothing less than that in the people you hang with. Sometimes being alone can be more fulfilling than being with the wrong friends.

A Fateful Friendship

S*erendipity* is one of my favorite words. It means "a fortunate accident." Fate, luck, destiny, whatever you call it—I
find it exciting, and in a strange way comforting, to think that
we might all be part of a "bigger plan," or at least play a role
in some smaller, everyday miracles.

Two years ago, when my relationship with my then-Best Friends Forever
(we even had BFF necklaces) took a
sudden and unexpected turn for the
worse, *serendipity* was the farthest
thing from my mind. The breakup was
an *accident,* surely. I spent weeks trying to figure out where I went wrong.

 **Seen It?**

In the romantic comedy
Serendipity (2001),
John Cusack's character
is desperate to show
that he and his love
interest, played by
Kate Beckinsale, are
fated to be together.

But *fortunate?* My tears argued otherwise. I had always felt
comfortable in my skin, but suddenly my BFFs were changing
and trying to get me to change with them. We had always
been able to tell each other everything, but suddenly I felt my
friends weren't really listening, except when using my words
to backstab me. We were once "the three *amigas,*" but now it
seemed like it was two against one, and I was always the *one.*
I had always been a peacekeeper, but suddenly we were bick-
ering constantly. Even though I wasn't a drama queen, I
started crying myself to sleep at night. I was being sucked
under in a whirlpool of turmoil, and one thing was certain—
I had to get out.

Everyone talks about "broken hearts" in a romantic aspect,
but nobody mentions how heartbreaking it is when friends
split up. I had other acquaintances, friends from class, people

to sit with at lunch, but it wasn't the same. Heather and Nadine had been the two sisters I never had. I missed them, even though I remembered how depressed I had been with them and how bad they were making me feel about myself. I had never lacked self-confidence, but now it was slipping away. Without my "two *amigas*," I felt miserable and utterly alone, like someone had changed the rules, and I didn't know how to play the game anymore.

Then one day, while I was feeling blue, Emma called me. Emma had been my best friend in middle school, and

HOW ABOUT YOU?

Do you **differentiate** between **best friends** and **BFF**s? What is it that makes one different from the other?

I still considered her one of my good friends, but we had grown apart the past few years. Even though we went to the same high school, we had different classes and different interests. Around the same time I met Heather and Nadine, Emma began to drift away, like a boat being pulled out to sea by a different current. I tried to keep up our friendship at first, but she was always too "busy" to hang out. My phone calls became less frequent and then almost nonexistent. Now, sitting in my bedroom listening to Emma's familiar voice on the other end of the phone, I realized how much I missed her.

"You've seemed sad lately," she said. "Are you okay?" Soon I found myself telling her everything, hiccupping with tears by the time I was done. Emma just listened. And then she said, "It's okay, Dallas. You'll always have me." I realized how selfish I

For Real?

Like love, **friendship** is a **universal** part of life. Here's how to say the word "friend" in different parts of the planet:

- Spanish: *amigo, amiga*
- French: *ami* • German: *freund*
- Italian: *amico, amica*
- Norwegian: *venn*

had been to let Emma drift away in the first place, and how lucky I was that she had paddled back to me.

Instantly, it was like old times. In fact, before long Emma and I were closer than ever. I rediscovered what it was like to have a friend who accepted me for me, who really listened when I talked, who I felt safe confiding in. I was happier than I'd been in months. Emma seemed happy, too, yet something wasn't quite right. It seemed as if she was still holding something back from me.

One night, as we lay side by side in our sleeping bags after a late-night movie marathon—including, of course, the best chick flick ever, *Serendipity*—Emma turned on her side and looked at me, her face glistening with tears. "There's something I've been wanting to tell you for a really long time," she said, taking a deep breath. "My sister is . . . anorexic."

I sat there, holding my best friend's hand as she poured out everything she had buried inside for so long. Her sadness, her fear, her frustration and anger and loneliness. I felt like someone had flushed

CONSIDER THIS . . .

Serendipity isn't the only great **chick flick** out there for sleepovers. Check out these great movies:

- *How to Lose a Guy in Ten Days* (2003)
- *You've Got Mail* (1998)
- *While You Were Sleeping* (1995)
- *When Harry Met Sally* (1989)
- *Bridget Jones's Diary* (2001)

the toilet while I was in a steaming-hot shower, suddenly shocking me with ice water. *How could I not have known? How could I not have seen that something was wrong?* All this time I had been so caught up in my own worries and troubles—things that didn't seem nearly so big anymore—that I hadn't even noticed Emma's world crumbling around her.

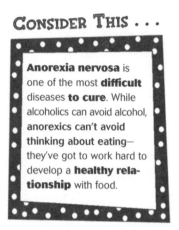

CONSIDER THIS . . .

Anorexia nervosa is one of the most **difficult** diseases **to cure**. While alcoholics can avoid alcohol, anorexics can't avoid thinking about eating— they've got to work hard to develop a **healthy relationship** with food.

It started two years ago, she explained between hiccups, about the same time she started drifting away from me. Other than a few phone calls, I had barely made an effort to pull her back in. "I'm sorry, Emma," I whispered, crying now myself. "I'm so, so sorry."

"I'm sorry I didn't tell you sooner," she said. "I knew you would listen. I just . . . I didn't know how to get the words out. But now I feel so much better, like I've been carrying around a backpack full of textbooks and suddenly God's given me a locker."

A month later, Emma's sister left home to go to an eating-disorder camp four hours away. Emma was beside herself with sadness, but at least this time she had me.

* * *

If you had told me two years ago that losing my BFF was an act of serendipity, I would have refused to listen. But the thing I've learned about fortunate accidents is that at first it's hard to get past the "accident" part. Oftentimes you have to look back through the lens of time to realize how fortunate you truly are. I see now that fate was smiling on me after all. My fallout with Heather and Nadine helped me find Emma again, and she showed me what a true friend is. Perhaps more important, losing my not-so-true friends allowed me to be there for Emma when she needed me the most.

Emma's sister is now doing much better, by the way. And our friendship is healthier than ever.

Dallas Nicole Woodburn, age 17

OUTSIDE THE BOX

It's just like the song says, "Breaking up is hard to do." When friendships end, it can be as dramatic as any other breakup. But it doesn't have to be. If you find yourself going through a breakup, here are some things to keep in mind to help you get through the weirdness of it all:

- Be open and honest about how you're feeling without being unnecessarily harsh.
- Avoid name-calling and shouting, even if you're feeling angry. Eventually, your emotions will simmer down, and you'll be glad you kept your cool.
- Deal with your emotions in a healthy way— write down in a journal how you're feeling to get it all out.

EVER HAVE ONE OF THOSE DAYS? You know the ones . . . you wake up on the wrong side of the bed, you're cranky, people aren't being nice to you, and nothing seems to go right? Yeah, me, too. In fact, last Thursday was one of the those days. Boy, was it a whopper!

As night rolled on, my sleep deprivation was getting to me, and I just really needed to hear the voice of my best friend. I looked at the clock. It was late. Really late for her, since she was on East Coast time and I was on the West Coast. But I knew she was some-what of a late-nighter, so I stepped out onto the front porch, dialed her number and waited.

As the phone rang, I waited anxiously for her to pick up. *Please be there. Please be there,* I said to myself. Five rings. Six rings. Seven rings. I was just about to give up when I heard her voice on the other end.

"Hello?"

I sighed in relief as I greeted her, so thankful to hear her voice, so thankful that she was there, so thankful that now I would be able to download my feelings and get much-needed sympathy and advice. Sometimes there's nothing like a best friend to talk with, even if it is through a telephone line.

Being a good listener is a skill, but it's one that you can learn. Here are some tips for being a good listener. Try practicing them every day and see how well you do!

- Don't interrupt the person talking.
- When she's through talking, count to three before speaking up. This way you make sure that the other person has completed her thought.
- Try to keep an open mind to what the other person is saying and don't judge her.
- Only offer advice if it's asked for . . . don't impose your ideas.
- If you're talking face-to-face, use eye contact.
- If you're talking on the phone, don't do other things like play a computer game or, do homework while you're listening. Give your friend your full attention.
- Keep people's secrets when they confide in you so you will be truly trustworthy.
- Let people know you're listening by providing reinforcement, like nodding your head or saying, "Uh huh."
- Try to empathize with what your friend's going through by putting yourself in her place and imagining how you would feel.

Guys Come, and Guys Go

The phone rings,
As I sit on the line,
Waiting for her to pick up,
Not worried about the time.

"Hello?" she asks,
Our conversation begins,
I really need to talk to her,
I need her to make me grin.

For Real?

Nearly **80%** of teens who are **sexually abused** don't tell their parents about it, while **70%** will tell a friend what happened.

"My heart is broken,"
My voice carries through the phone,
"Why did it turn out this way?"
She lets me know I'm not alone.

We talk for hours,
About guys, about life,
We talk about our stress,
And discuss our recent strife.

We share our funny secrets,
Tell each other everything,
Turn to each other for the support we need,
An explanation we need not bring.

Best friends don't need to ask,
They always seem to know,
You listen, they listen,
That's just the way it goes.

The bond of
    friendship,
Cannot be broken
    easily,
A true friend is
    irreplaceable,
I'm sure you can
    agree.

Guys come, and
    guys go,
Hearts break, and
    tears fall,
But never forget that
    your best friend,
Will be with you
    through it all.

Stephanie Ives,
    age 16

WHERE DO YOU STAND?

When your friends turn to you for help, are you a good listener?

Your friend calls in the middle of your favorite show. You . . .
A. call her back when your show's over.
B. turn off the TV and tune in to her.

Your friend always complains about the same thing, and you're tired of her not taking your advice. You . . .
A. tune her out—you've heard it all before.
B. listen to her situation with fresh ears.

You don't like your friend's boyfriend, so it's hard when she calls to complain about him. You . . .
A convince her to dump him—he's no good for her anyway.
B empathize by putting yourself in her situation.

Your BFF has started acting anorexic. You don't get it—she's much skinnier than you are. You . . .
A get frustrated when she wants to talk about it.
B listen to her without making judgments.

Your friend finally shares something with you, and you're dying to tell her how you really feel. You . . .
A interrupt her before she gets going—you know what she's going to say anyway.
B let her finish talking before jumping in.

How'd ya do?
Mostly As = Your listening skills could use some refining.
Mostly Bs = You're a great listener!

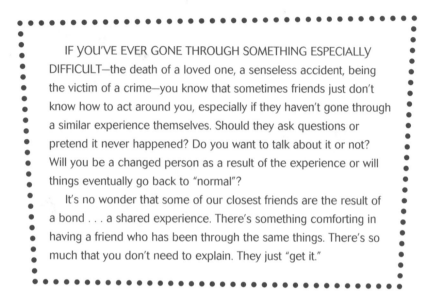

IF YOU'VE EVER GONE THROUGH SOMETHING ESPECIALLY DIFFICULT—the death of a loved one, a senseless accident, being the victim of a crime—you know that sometimes friends just don't know how to act around you, especially if they haven't gone through a similar experience themselves. Should they ask questions or pretend it never happened? Do you want to talk about it or not? Will you be a changed person as a result of the experience or will things eventually go back to "normal"?

It's no wonder that some of our closest friends are the result of a bond . . . a shared experience. There's something comforting in having a friend who has been through the same things. There's so much that you don't need to explain. They just "get it."

Take Back the Night

We met under unfortunate circumstances—in a girls' group for survivors of sexual abuse. Her name was Kimmy, and she was twelve years old. I was thirteen. While there were six other girls in the group, Kimmy and I immediately connected and began sharing with each other. I had a connection with her that was unlike any with my other friends—we both were survivors of sexual abuse.

For the next five months, Kimmy and I met weekly at our group. We shared many laughs and long talks, and participated in activities with all the other girls. Outside our group, Kimmy

THE WORD

Sexual abuse is defined as any kind of sexual situation **involving a child** and an **older person**.

and I had sleepovers together. Kimmy opened up to me and shared the details of what she went through. She invited me to her birthday party, while I invited her to spend time with me at my summer house. Our group eventually had to come to an end, but it was just the beginning of our friendship.

CONSIDER THIS . . .

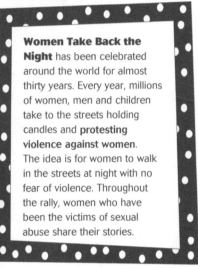

Women Take Back the Night has been celebrated around the world for almost thirty years. Every year, millions of women, men and children take to the streets holding candles and **protesting violence against women**. The idea is for women to walk in the streets at night with no fear of violence. Throughout the rally, women who have been the victims of sexual abuse share their stories.

Kimmy was always a phone call away. There were many nights I needed someone to listen to me, and she was always there. Together we experienced sixteenth birthday parties, getting our driver's licenses, boyfriends . . . even getting together with other girls from our girls' group. Although we went to different high schools, it never affected our friendship.

Before long, it was time to graduate high school. My graduation party was held at my summer house in Wisconsin. Dozens of friends showed up for the big day, including Kimmy. When we talked about college, we were shocked to find out that we'd both decided on the same university.

Today Kimmy and I attend college together, building more memories and often looking back on how our friendship began in such unusual circumstances. We find ourselves laughing at

 **Seen It?**

Beverly Hills 90210 featured an episode where Kelly and Steve participate in a **Take Back the Night** rally at California University.

Address Book

If **you** or a **friend** are a **victim** of **sexual abuse**, you can turn to the National Abuse, Rape and Incest Hotline at **1-800-656-HOPE**.

some of the childish things we did when we were younger.

In October 2004, Kim and I took part in Take Back the Night at our university. The night is for survivors of sexual assault and others to go out and take to the streets, chanting powerful words about being survivors and bringing awareness to sexual violence. To my amazement, Kimmy and I were asked to lead the march. With hundreds of people behind us, Kimmy and I held two lit torches and marched into the night. Every now and then we looked over at each other, smiling, knowing just how far we had both come in life.

I believe that everything happens for a reason. If Kimmy and I had never gone through the difficult things that we had, our paths would never have crossed. In some ways, I see my past as a blessing. Kimmy is one of those blessings . . . a friend I will hold close to my heart forever.

Erin Merryn, age 20

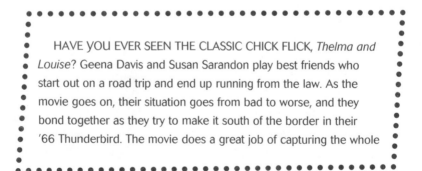

HAVE YOU EVER SEEN THE CLASSIC CHICK FLICK, *Thelma and Louise*? Geena Davis and Susan Sarandon play best friends who start out on a road trip and end up running from the law. As the movie goes on, their situation goes from bad to worse, and they bond together as they try to make it south of the border in their '66 Thunderbird. The movie does a great job of capturing the whole "us versus the world" thing. Thelma and Louise are so close as friends and so caught up in what's happening to them that they stop being able to see things clearly. Rationality flies out the window as they get closer and closer in a pact to keep their pride and dignity and to remain ever loyal to each other.

Seen It?

In the movie *Girl Interrupted* (1999), Winona Ryder and Angelina Jolie develop an intense and dangerous relationship while in a teen mental institution.

I won't tell you how the movie ends in case you haven't seen it, but let's just say that there are times when relationships become so close that they can actually become dangerous. When you and your friend go through a crisis together, it's all too easy to lose objectivity and become the "us" against the world.

Becoming One and Losing a Half

I started my first year of high school knowing most of my classmates, but I heard through the grapevine about a new girl from out of town who was possibly bulimic. In the past, I had gone through some challenging personal problems of my own, so I immediately felt a bond with the new girl. I let her know that if she needed someone to talk with that I was available.

For Real?

Teens spend an average of **7.7 hours** each week talking on the **phone**.

In no time, we were inseparable. We spent hours on the phone and wouldn't go anywhere without the

CONSIDER THIS . . .

If you're **keeping** a painful **secret**, getting it off your chest by sharing it with a friend can be a great thing. Not only will you be doing yourself a favor by lightening the weight you're carrying around, but you'll also be letting the world know that you're ready for help.

other. When you heard her name spoken, mine was usually the one that followed, and vice versa. We did everything together and confided everything to each other. She told me that she was bulimic and anorexic, and I told her that I had a problem with cutting. She admitted to having a problem with that, too. With everything we learned, we became more and more attached, more like one person instead of two. We felt each other's pain and emotions and could understand each other so well. We leaned on one another to get through the days without self-destructing. And when we'd find each other engaging in negative behavior, we would stop each other, even though we were being so hypocritical because we kept doing it ourselves.

One day during biology, my friend was acting very depressed. She said she wanted to end her life. I could tell she wasn't joking. We had been passing notes back and forth, and she was writing down her feelings when she

Read It?

The novel *My Sister's Bones* by Cathi Hanauer is about the effects of an **eating disorder**, not only on the one **starving** herself, but also on everyone around her.

jumped up and ran out of class. I ran down the hallway after her. I just knew she was serious. I followed her to the stairwell where I grabbed her and hugged her tightly. I was shaking, and so was she—I had never been so scared in my life.

Things didn't get any better after that. I always found myself running after my friend and holding her down when

Address Book

For more information and a listing by state of places to reach out for help when it comes to **eating disorders**, check out www.teenanorexiabulimia.org.

all she wanted to do was make herself throw up. I couldn't let her go . . . I loved her too much. Living without her was not an option. If she would go, so would I. We swore to it.

After returning from a two-week vacation, I saw that my friend was skinnier than ever. She looked like she had lost half of herself. I was terrified and knew that she needed to be somewhere full-time—she wasn't going to get any better at school or home. I convinced her to consider going to a hospital, and for a while she was okay with it.

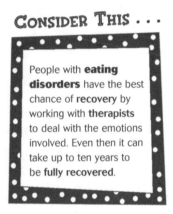

CONSIDER THIS . . .

People with **eating disorders** have the best chance of **recovery** by working with **therapists** to deal with the emotions involved. Even then it can take up to ten years to be **fully recovered**.

Then one day she didn't show up at school, and I had a bad feeling. Immediately, I called her house, and she picked up, sounding horribly sick. She hadn't eaten and had thrown up so much that it became blood instead of food. I was so scared. I didn't want to tell her mom because I knew my friend would be angry, but it had become too dangerous. One of the teachers drove me to her house. I couldn't stop crying and hugging her when I got there. Eventually, her mom came home and spoke to a teacher about finding a place to admit her so she could get the help she needed.

She found an outpatient program, but still didn't come to school for a full month. At first, she was angry with me because she felt I had turned her in. I knew that she would be, but losing her would have been worse. For the month she was gone, I didn't know how to cope with not having a part of me in school. She had become half of my mind and body, and I'd become half of her. It was scary how empty and lost I felt. I had no energy and couldn't concentrate.

The day she came back, I didn't know what to do or say, but she gave me the biggest hug, and I started crying all over. The connection we had and still have today is unbreakable. Our psychologist couldn't understand our bond, but knew it was dangerous to be taking on each other's pain the way we were. To this day, even though she is not in the same school as me, I love her and care about her so much. Not seeing her every day is difficult. While she used to be my other half, I'm now complete on my own, but all of me still loves her. I want her to know that I will be there for her forever, through any challenges. We will face them together.

Orly Shoshana,
age 16

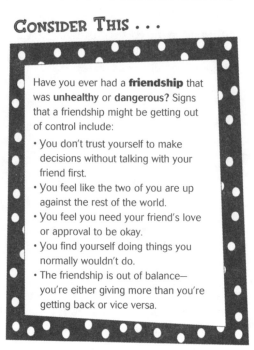

CONSIDER THIS . . .

Have you ever had a **friendship** that was **unhealthy** or **dangerous?** Signs that a friendship might be getting out of control include:

• You don't trust yourself to make decisions without talking with your friend first.
• You feel like the two of you are up against the rest of the world.
• You feel you need your friend's love or approval to be okay.
• You find yourself doing things you normally wouldn't do.
• The friendship is out of balance— you're either giving more than you're getting back or vice versa.

JESSE, A GIRL IN MY DORM FRESHMAN YEAR OF COLLEGE, had a secret, and she kept it hidden very well. I was clueless about it. After all, most girls I knew chowed down on comfort food every now and then. I never thought anything of it when I'd see Jesse sitting on her bed, studying and wolfing down an entire box of chocolate-chip cookies. I myself spent all-nighters dining on Diet Coke and Nacho Cheese Doritos. But one night I came home from the library and found Jesse crying uncontrollably in the bathroom, and she spilled her guts and told me that she was bulimic. I was in shock.

For Real?

Bulimia should be taken seriously. **10%** of girls and boys who are bulimic will eventually **die** as a result, either from starvation, medical complications or suicide.

I had never known anyone who was bulimic, and I knew I was not equipped to handle the situation on my own. I convinced Jesse that telling the resident advisor, an older student who was kind of like the mother hen of our dorm, was the way to go. I promised to go with her. So later that night, we sat down with the RA and figured out what needed to happen.

I'm so glad that Jesse confided in me that night. I could tell that getting her secret off her chest was a tremendous relief. Although Jesse eventually transferred to a school closer to home and we lost touch, I feel hopeful that the night she shared her secret with me was the beginning of her road to recovery.

Julie

It was early October 2003. My friend Julie and I were on our way to school. We rode in the same carpool. We were very good friends. We wrote notes so no one would listen to our conversations. Sometimes we wrote our deepest secrets. We would joke around. I remember some days we would skip class for fifteen minutes just to talk. Those were good old days.

Then one day Julie was acting depressed. She said something to me that I didn't think I would ever hear from her. She wrote in a note that she wanted to kill herself. I didn't know what to do or what to say to her. She said she had tried to hurt herself many times. She showed me her wrists. Cut marks were all over them. I asked why she did it. She didn't tell me. I told her that since I knew what was going on, I would have to tell somebody. She didn't even care. She thought the more people that knew about it, the better.

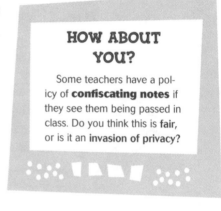

HOW ABOUT YOU?

Some teachers have a policy of **confiscating notes** if they see them being passed in class. Do you think this is **fair**, or is it an **invasion of privacy**?

Seen It?

In *Pretty in Pink* (1986), Molly Ringwald's **crush** is **revealed** to all when the note she passes in class is intercepted by the boy she likes.

When I got out of the car, I immediately went to see my school counselor and told her what was going on. Right away she went to get Julie, and I didn't see her in class for the rest of the day. The next day,

CONSIDER THIS . . .

When a **friend** is doing something that could potentially **put her life at risk**, you might feel conflicted about getting an adult involved. **Don't.** Your friend might be upset at first, but in the long run, she'll thank you for caring enough to stand up for her.

Julie wasn't in school—she was told to stay home for a day. I was very worried about what she might be doing at home—it could be anything.

When Julie came back to school, she told me that she wouldn't talk about suicide or anything close to it again. I hoped that she wouldn't. I kept going to my counselor—I couldn't stop thinking about Julie. A week later, I saw that Julie had more cut marks on her wrist, but these were even bigger and deeper than before. I don't like tattling, but when something this serious was going on, I knew I had to tell someone.

My school counselor and I went to get Julie. We talked for ten minutes, and then I was told to go back to class. I hugged Julie good-bye. That was the last time I ever saw her. An hour later the police and paramedics came and took Julie away. Sometimes I ask myself, *Why? Why did I tattle? I am a complete idiot!* Then I remember that I kept my friend from doing something stupid.

Jay Sirach, age 19

HOW ABOUT YOU?

Does doing the **responsible** thing by trying to **prevent** someone from getting hurt or hurting herself make you a tattletale?

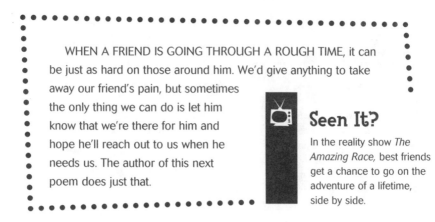

WHEN A FRIEND IS GOING THROUGH A ROUGH TIME, it can be just as hard on those around him. We'd give anything to take away our friend's pain, but sometimes the only thing we can do is let him know that we're there for him and hope he'll reach out to us when he needs us. The author of this next poem does just that.

Seen It?

In the reality show *The Amazing Race,* best friends get a chance to go on the adventure of a lifetime, side by side.

My Dear Friend

My dear friend,
please don't cry.
I'm here for you,
and that's no lie.

My dear friend,
you can do something amazing with your life.
Please stop ruining yourself
with that stupid knife.

My dear friend,
without you I'd never see the light of day.
I can name about a hundred
people who feel the same way.

My dear friend,
things don't always go right.

But I know you're strong,
and you can win this fight.

My dear friend,
this road takes us on such a long ride.
But no matter what,
I'll always be by your side.

Raquel Dominguez, age 16

Do you have a friend who's going through a
difficult time? Here are some tips for being
a rock-solid support:

- Let your friend know that you're there for
  her and that your goal is to help her however
  you can.
- Listen, listen, listen. Make sure your friend
  has your ear whenever she needs it.
- Don't judge; offer advice only when and if
  it is asked for.
- Be patient . . . don't expect your friend to
  bounce back and be herself right away.
- Do something special and unexpected for your
  friend!

Spotlight On . . . TURNING TO
FRIENDS IN TIMES OF NEED

One of the best things about having friends you trust and rely on is that when you need help, they're there for you. Friends can be invaluable resources when dealing with heavy stuff, like divorce and other family problems, personal issues, like depression and low self-esteem, or the death or injury of a loved one.

The trouble is, sometimes friends just don't know how to help. In fact, the only person who really knows what will help you get through a tough time is you, and you might not even be sure. Don't expect your BFF to be a mind reader or know exactly what to do. Here's what you can do:

- Let your friend know what you need from him or her most, whether it's space, a hug or something more tangible.
- Be honest with your friend if her efforts are making things harder on you.
- Remember that your friends have the best intentions, even if they're not hitting the mark.
- Be patient with your friends and with yourself . . . don't expect problems to get solved overnight.
- When you're through your crisis, let your friend know how much you appreciate her being there for you, and return the favor when your friend is the one in need.

JONI MITCHELL WROTE A SONG CALLED "BIG YELLOW TAXI" that was redone by The Counting Crows. My favorite line is that familiar saying, "You don't know what you've got 'til it's gone." Why do I love that line so much? Because it's *so true*. We rarely stop to appreciate the people in our lives while they're here because we somehow just get used to them. And the weird thing is, the closer people are to us—best friends, family members—the more we seem to take them for granted. We figure they'll always be around, so why make a big deal out of it?

But what if they aren't always around? What if something happens, and one of those people in your life whom you love so much tragically disappears? Would you vow never to take another friend for granted ever again? To always let the people you love know how you feel about them?

This next author got a wake-up call with her own best friend, but luckily she had an opportunity to show just how much she cares before it was too late.

CONSIDER THIS

It's easy to take things and people for **granted** . . . all of us are **guilty of it** at some time or another. Perhaps that's because we always think that something or someone better is just around the corner. What do you think?

WHERE DO YOU STAND?

Do you know how to lean on friends when you're in a tough spot? Would you turn to a friend for help in one of these situations?

❏ YES ❏ NO   You have been feeling really down lately, and nothing has been able to snap you out of your mood.

❏ YES ❏ NO   Your dad loses his job, and you're worried about finances at home.

❏ YES ❏ NO   You find out that your brother has been binge drinking at parties, and you're worried about him.

❏ YES ❏ NO   Your teacher says something to you that makes you uncomfortable. You think it's harassment, but don't know how to handle it.

❏ YES ❏ NO   Your cat dies, and you are beyond sad, but you're not sure that your friend would understand why it's hitting you so hard.

Paying Back a Friend

September 28, 2001, was the worst day of my life.

Stephanie and I have been the closest of friends for ten years. She means everything to me—I can always rely on her for help. She offers me a shoulder to cry on, but more important, she can make me laugh. Until this date, I had taken our friendship for granted . . . she had always been there for me. Now I finally got the chance to be there for her.

Usually, Steffi and I spend the entire weekends together just watching TV and eating chips (we call them "Debbi-Steffi weekends"). That Friday, however, I took a trip with my family, and Steffi went to a sweet-sixteen party. Late Saturday night when I returned, my phone rang. It was Steffi's mom.

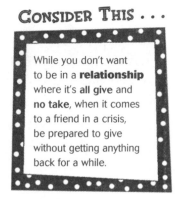

CONSIDER THIS . . .

While you don't want to be in a **relationship** where it's **all give** and **no take**, when it comes to a friend in a crisis, be prepared to give without getting anything back for a while.

"Steffi got into an accident," she said. I felt suspended in time while life whirled around me.

"She'll be in surgery all night," her mom continued, "but she told me to tell you that she loves you." Reality struck, and I broke down, sobbing into the receiver. All that came out through my tears was, "OhmyGodohmyGodohmyGod."

"Pray for her," she told me.

"I love her . . . I love her so much," I whispered.

I lay in bed that night, unable to sleep. Scenes from our friendship paraded through my mind. I saw our memories slipping away before my eyes—our six years at summer camp together, all the "Debbi-Steffi weekends," decorating our rooms with drawings we made for each other, singing over the phone, and going to concerts and movies. I relived the time we walked, laughing, through a blizzard to the Wawa to buy cookies. I saw us sitting together at Starbucks, doing homework and enjoying cappuccinos. I recalled our working together at the Centenary College radio station, and how we told Steffi's father to call and request songs. Now, I was terrified that Steffi was going to die.

For Real?

Is **Starbucks** taking over the planet? **Every single day,** three Starbucks stores open up somewhere in the world.

I found out the following day that Steffi was badly hurt, but I sensed she was going to be all right. As soon as she was allowed visitors, I went to see her at the hospital. When I first saw her lying there, bruised and in pain, I was simply relieved to see her alive. It was frightening to hear that she had endured an operation lasting several hours to insert a rod into her broken arm. What scared me even more, however, was the fact that Steffi had no memory of that night or of the accident. "Why was I even on that road?" she wondered aloud.

For Real?
Have you ever visited a friend in the hospital? How did it make you feel?

I visited Steffi every day for the two weeks that she remained hospitalized. Each time I walked into her room and saw the smile appear on her face, I knew that she needed me there. I was finally able to repay her for the joy her friendship had given me all these years. I told her I would be there every step of the way, and I was determined to keep my promise. Parents and teachers tried to dissuade me from spending so much time at the hospital, but nothing else seemed important. I didn't care that schoolwork and college applications awaited my attention. I couldn't concentrate on anything else—Stephanie was all that mattered.

When Stephanie returned home, she continued to heal. She gradually recovered, but the effect of her accident still lingers to this day. It has made me realize that a good friendship is the most precious thing in life, and I will now value my bond with Steffi above anything else. We have been through so much together, and her accident has brought us only closer. I could not imagine my life without Stephanie, and I know we will always be the best of friends.

Debbi Rotkowitz, age 20

If you've got a friend in the hospital who you want to visit, follow these steps to make your visit as helpful and fun as possible:

- If you're worried about timing, call first and make sure your friend is up to the visit.
- Bring messages from friends and classmates in the forms of cards, audiotapes and home movies.
- Grab some of your friend's favorite things from home, such as clothes, a favorite book or makeup, to make him or her feel more comfortable.
- Don't let the TV distract you. Turn it off!
- If your friend can ride in a wheelchair, see if you can take him or her out for a ride or to get some fresh air.
- Do things to distract your friend—read a book together or play a card game.
- Be cheerful and happy . . . moods can be contagious!
- If your friend can eat normal food, bring a favorite candy bar or other treat.

WHAT WOULD HAPPEN IF YOUR FRIEND WAS ALWAYS CALLING YOU, but you never bothered to call her back? What if your friend saw you through a difficult situation at home, but when he was struggling with a personal problem, you were too caught up with your own life to deal with his? My guess is that the friendship wouldn't be around much longer.

Surprise! Friendships take work. To be a good friend you have to return those phone calls. You have to be there for a friend when he's going through a rough time. You have to step up to the plate when it's needed, and you have to know how to let your friend step up and help you in return. But it's worth it. When you have a friend who knows he can count on you, and you feel the same in return, you can get through anything.

CONSIDER THIS . . .

Receiving gifts and things from friends is a great thing, but they're not nearly as important as the **emotional gifts** a friend can share— **support, trust, honesty** and **love**.

The Little Things Friends Do

The only way to have a friend is to *be* a friend. I once read that and have (for the most part) always stuck by it. In my opinion, it's a rule that is key to keeping any friendship. Now to follow this rule, you don't have to give your friends the moon and the stars; you just have to do things to show you care, to show you love them, to show that you're there for them. You know . . . the little things friends do.

For as long as I could remember, Rebecca had been there

Read It?

The *Harry Potter* series by J. K. Rowling and the movies based on it made wearing glasses cool among kids again because Harry wears glasses with black circular frames.

for me. From something as small as a bad mark on a test, to something as big as coping with death, she was there, caring when it seemed no one else did, drying my eyes or just listening when I needed someone to talk to. Little did I know that Rebecca was about to need a friend more than I ever had.

The date was March 22, five days after Rebecca's birthday. The rain pelted down furiously as my mother and I drove home from the grocery store.

"I'm not getting glasses! I don't care if they're only for school. I'll look ugly! None of my friends have them! I won't wear them anyway!" I cried to my mom. Earlier that day, I had gotten my eyes tested and was told that I needed glasses. I was so upset because, despite what my mom said, I knew that glasses looked horrible on me! Thoughts of my friends laughing at me and talking about me behind my back were all I could think of. I knew deep down that my health was more important than how I looked, but a bigger part of me cared too much about what other people would think.

When I got home, I wiped my eyes and ran up to my room where I picked up the phone to check who had called. There were about twenty calls waiting for me. What

CONSIDER THIS . . .

Would you rather wear **contact lenses** than **glasses** because you think they **look lame?** Many **celebrities,** including Britney Spears, Jennifer Aniston and Julia Roberts, have actually worn glasses not because they need them, but because they **think** they **look cool!**

could have happened during the hour I was gone that could be so important? I was about to call my friend to see what was going on when the phone started to ring. It was my friend Maria.

What she told me was something that I never thought I would hear.

"Becca just called me," her muffled, crying voice said. I didn't speak. *What had happened?* My heart became a fist, pounding at my chest, each beat louder than the last.

> ### For Real?
> Only ten years ago, having their own phone line was a big deal for teens. Today, **75%** of **teens** don't need them . . . they've got their own **cell phones**.

Maria went on. "Kelsey got her test back. She has cancer. Becca's at the hospital with her now."

The news stabbed me like a knife. The phone fell from my hand, leaving me shaking and cold. Kelsey is Rebecca's sister, and she's only a year younger than us. I've known her since I was five. Kelsey could always make me laugh and was not only Becca's sister, but my friend as well. Tears rolled down my cheeks like lava pouring out of a volcano. I couldn't breathe.

How? How had this happened? I knew it happened to kids, but the only people I knew who ever got diagnosed with leukemia were adults. This couldn't be happening. It must be a dream, and soon I

CONSIDER THIS . . .

The **Team in Training** (*www.teamintraining.org*) is the **world's largest** endurance sports training program. Athletes sign up to train for marathons and bike races to **raise money** for **leukemia** and **lymphoma treatment** and **research**.

would wake up to a world where the biggest issue of the day was my having to get glasses. But that didn't happen. Life from that day forward changed, especially for Becca.

Two days later, Rebecca came back to school. I walked up to her and threw my arms around her. I told her that if she ever needed anything, she could let me know. A single tear rolled down my cheek. She took the news as well as could be expected—day by day. Some days Kelsey was, well . . . Kelsey! She made us laugh, and she was happy and full of life. Other days it was as if she was a different person—pale, sad . . . just not the Kelsey I knew. Luckily, she had more good days than bad, and she could always manage to keep a smile.

THE WORD

Chemotherapy is drug **treatment** for **cancer**. It works by preventing the dividing of cancer cells. Unfortunately, it also tends to attack the cells on the scalp and in the stomach, causing temporary baldness and nausea.

That summer I wrote Becca a lot of poems that made her laugh, even if they had nothing to do with her sister. I loved making her happy because she has always done the same for me. She has a book full of all the poems that I've ever written for her, and when I read them, I feel like I've given her at least a fraction of the support, love and guidance that she's given me over the years. And by the way—Kelsey is doing great now, and hopefully things will stay that way!

- *March 22, 2004:* The day that Kelsey was diagnosed with leukemia.
- *March 22, 2004:* The day I forgot about my own troubles and thought about someone else's.

• *March 22, 2004:* The day I decided to start doing more of the little things friends do.

Erin Shea, age 12

Spotlight On . . . LEUKEMIA

Leukemia is a cancer that affects the white blood cells of the body. Children with leukemia produce abnormal white blood cells, which are unable to fight disease the way normal white blood cells would. When leukemia does affect a child, it tends to develop rapidly in the body, making it harder to cure.

Leukemia is more common in children than most other forms of cancer, but it still affects only about 2,200 children each year. It is more common among boys than girls, and among white children than children of other ethnic groups.

Chemotherapy is the most common form of treatment for leukemia, and sometimes radiation treatment is used, too. Even when the cancer has been treated and goes into remission (that means the cancer is gone from the cells in the body), chemotherapy usually goes on for a few years to make sure the cancer doesn't come back.

Take the Quiz:
DO YOU KNOW HOW
TO HELP A FRIEND

1. Your BFF has been feeling under the weather for some time now, and she's finally gone to the doctor. The diagnosis surprises you both . . . she has lupus, an immune disorder that can sometimes be fatal. What do you do?

___ A. You are overwhelmed by your own feelings of sadness and, frankly, being around your friend is too difficult right now. Besides, she's got bigger things to worry about than you.

___ B. You don't really know how to handle this, so you decide to pretend that everything is just fine and normal. Distraction is the best strategy.

___ C. You ask your friend what you can do to help and read up on everything you can about lupus. You're going to make sure that she doesn't go through this alone.

2. You're having an IM discussion with your friend late one night. At first, you're joking around, but then she says some things about being seriously depressed, and you realize she's not trying to be funny . . . she's sharing a dark secret with you. What do you do next?

___ A. You stop responding to the IM, pretending that you've stepped away from the computer. You're caught off guard and don't know what to say.

___ B. You try to make light of it and change the subject ASAP. You're not prepared to have this conversation right now. If she really needs to talk about it, she'll bring it up in person.

___ C. You talk with your friend over IM as long as she wants to keep confiding in you. The next day at school, you sit down with your friend and have a heart to heart about what's really going on.

3. You and your BFF both work at a burger joint together. You notice your friend is a big flirt with all the guys there, so you are surprised when she tells you that the line cook sexually harassed her. How do you respond?

____ A. You doubt her story, especially considering her history of flirting. You roll your eyes and decide that she's just using this as a ploy to get attention.

____ B. You listen to her talk and try to suggest that maybe what happened wasn't what she thought. You give her advice about how to handle it if it happens again.

____ C. You know that harassment needs to be taken seriously, and if that's what your friend feels happened, then that's what happened. You go with her to fill in the manager on what's going on.

4. One of the guys in your circle of friends loses his father in a car accident. You've never experienced a loss like this before, so you aren't sure how to handle it. What do you do?

____ A. You feel bad for doing it, but you find yourself avoiding any contact with the friend. You just don't have a clue about what to say to him and figure he probably wants to be alone.

____ B. You try to hang out with your friend like everything's normal, asking him once how he's doing and then leaving it at that when he says he's doing okay.

____ C. While you can't relate, you can put yourself in your friend's situation and know that he must be in terrible pain. You write him a note to tell him that you're thinking about him and ask him to lean on you for support whenever he needs to.

5. Your friend is dumped by the guy she's been obsessed with for the past year. You are secretly happy because you have never really approved of the whole relationship, especially since she was usually too busy hanging out with her beau instead of with you. How do you help her?

___ A. You burst out and tell her how unhealthy the relationship was in the first place and that she's lucky to be out of it. You suggest double-dating with two other guys the upcoming weekend.

___ B. You've been through heartache before, so you tell her what worked for you to get over it and suggest she do the same.

___ C. Even though you didn't like the guy, you can see that your friend is really hurting. You offer to sleep over on Saturday so you can talk and distract each other, just like old times.

So, how good are you at helping friends? Give yourself 10 points for every A, 20 points for every B, and 30 points for every C.

50–70 points = Your "helping a friend" skills could use some brushing up. Most of the time, you're too caught up in your own thing to dig deep and feel another person's pain, or you're too scared of not knowing the right way to handle something. First, try working on your listening techniques . . . if you really start to hear your friend, you'll discover how best to help him.

80–120 points = You have the right intention when it comes to helping a friend, but your execution could use a little work. Don't feel as though you have to solve everything. Instead, try to meet your friend where he or she is and discover what she really needs from you . . . and then give it to her!

130–150 points = You're a great listener, and it shows in everything you do. You're definitely the person friends turn to in a crisis because they know that you'll give of yourself to be there for them, whether or not it's difficult.

EPILOGUE

WELL, THERE YOU GO . . . our humble offering of insight into the friends who make up your lives. We hope that this book spoke to you and gave you a fresh way to approach friendship challenges, encouraged you to make new friends, inspired you to be a better friend, or maybe even gave you the kick in the butt you needed to get out of an unhealthy friendship.

A wise person once said that friends are like chocolate chips in the cookie of life. And it's true—without friends our lives would be bland . . . boring . . . with no real "oomph." That's why it's a good thing that no matter what your situation— maybe you're in between best friends at the moment or maybe you've got a posse bigger than Diddy—these amazing people will continue to enter your life wherever you go. Some will pop in for a week or two and some will be there for every little milestone as the years go by. Just be the best friend you can be to those around you and you're sure to find yourself surrounded by people who make you laugh, root for you and catch you when you fall.

SUPPORTING OTHERS

MIND ON THE MEDIA (*www.motm.org*) is a non-profit organization concerned about sexist stereotypes in all forms of mass media. It creates positive change by teaching kids and adults media literacy, helping them gain the critical thinking skills they need to transform themselves from passive media consumers to savvy media analysts.

MOTM sponsors **Turn Beauty Inside Out** (TBIO), a national annual campaign that engages thousands of people in grassroots media education and activism. TBIO was created by *New Moon: The Magazine for Girls and Their Dreams*® almost five years ago, which also promotes positive self-image among youth. Fed up with the lie that beauty is only skin deep, *New Moon: The Magazine for Girls and Their Dreams*® is shattering ordinary beauty ideals by publishing its May–June "25 Beautiful Girls" issue. The Girls Editorial Board says, "Girls get so much pressure to be 'beautiful' on the outside. We want to get to know the whole girl—girls who care strongly about something and about themselves, girls who can overcome something, even if it's really hard."

The highlight of the campaign is the annual Girls Leadership Conference for girls ages 8–16 and their parents/mentors (from all over the U.S.). The event takes place in Los Angeles, New York City or Washington, D.C., focusing on representations of girls and women in film and TV, music, advertising and politics.

For complete information on the TBIO Leadership Conference and Mind on the Media, contact:

Mind on the Media
710 St. Olaf Ave. Ste. 200
Northfield, MN 55057
Phone: 952-210-1625
www.tbio.org

Who Is JACK CANFIELD?

Jack Canfield is one of America's leading experts in the development of human potential and personal effectiveness. He is both a dynamic, entertaining speaker and a highly sought-after trainer. Jack has a wonderful ability to inform and inspire audiences toward increased levels of self-esteem and peak performance. Jack most recently released a book for success entitled *The Success Principles: How to Get from Where You Are to Where You Want to Be.*

He is the author and narrator of several bestselling audio- and video-cassette programs, including *Self-Esteem and Peak Performance, How to Build High Self-Esteem, Self-Esteem in the Classroom* and *Chicken Soup for the Soul—Live.* He is regularly seen on television shows such as *Good Morning America, 20/20* and *NBC Nightly News.* Jack has coauthored numerous books, including the *Chicken Soup for the Soul* series, *Dare to Win* and *The Aladdin Factor* (all with Mark Victor Hansen), *100 Ways to Build Self-Concept in the Classroom* (with Harold C. Wells), *Heart at Work* (with Jacqueline Miller) and *The Power of Focus* (with Les Hewitt and Mark Victor Hansen).

Jack is a regularly featured speaker for professional associations, school districts, government agencies, churches, hospitals, sales organizations and corporations. His clients have included the American Dental Association, the American Management Association, AT&T, Campbell's Soup, Clairol, Domino's Pizza, GE, Hartford Insurance, ITT, Johnson & Johnson, the Million Dollar Roundtable, NCR, New England Telephone, Re/Max, Scott Paper, TRW and Virgin Records. Jack has taught on the faculty of Income Builders International, a school for entrepreneurs.

Jack conducts an annual seven-day training called Breakthrough to Success. It attracts entrepreneurs, educators, counselors, parenting trainers, corporate trainers, professional speakers, ministers and others interested in improving their lives and lives of others.

For free gifts from Jack and information on all his material and availability go to:

www.jackcanfield.com
Self-Esteem Seminars
P.O. Box 30880
Santa Barbara, CA 93130
phone: 805-563-2935 • fax: 805-563-2945

Who Is MARK VICTOR HANSEN?

In the area of human potential, no one is more respected than Mark Victor Hansen. For more than thirty years, Mark has focused solely on helping people from all walks of life reshape their personal vision of what's possible. His powerful messages of possibility, opportunity and action have created powerful change in thousands of organizations and millions of individuals worldwide.

He is a sought-after keynote speaker, bestselling author and marketing maven. Mark's credentials include a lifetime of entrepreneurial success and an extensive academic background. He is a prolific writer with many bestselling books, such as *The One Minute Millionaire, The Power of Focus, The Aladdin Factor* and *Dare to Win,* in addition to the *Chicken Soup for the Soul* series. Mark has made a profound influence through his library of audios, videos and articles in the areas of big thinking, sales achievement, wealth building, publishing success, and personal and professional development.

Mark is the founder of the MEGA Seminar Series. MEGA Book Marketing University and Building Your MEGA Speaking Empire are annual conferences where Mark coaches and teaches new and aspiring authors, speakers and experts on building lucrative publishing and speaking careers. Other MEGA events include MEGA Marketing Magic and My MEGA Life.

He has appeared on television (*Oprah,* CNN and *The Today Show*), in print (*Time, U.S. News & World Report, USA Today, New York Times* and *Entrepreneur*) and on countless radio interviews, assuring our planet's people that, "You can easily create the life you deserve."

As a philanthropist and humanitarian, Mark works tirelessly for organizations such as Habitat for Humanity, American Red Cross, March of Dimes, Childhelp USA and many others. He is the recipient of numerous awards that honor his entrepreneurial spirit, philanthropic heart and business acumen. He is a lifetime member of the Horatio Alger Association of Distinguished Americans, an organization that honored Mark with the prestigious Horatio Alger Award for his extraordinary life achievements.

Mark Victor Hansen is an enthusiastic crusader of what's possible and is driven to make the world a better place.

Mark Victor Hansen & Associates, Inc.
P.O. Box 7665
Newport Beach, CA 92658
phone: 949-764-2640
fax: 949-722-6912
Visit Mark online at: *www.markvictorhansen.com*

Who Is DEBORAH REBER?

Deborah is a former children's television executive who now writes for teens and tweens, most recently coauthoring *Chicken Soup for the Teenage Soul's The Real Deal: School* and writing the first books in a new series for PBS's teen Web site, *It's My Life* and Nickelodeon's tween girl property, *EverGirl.* Deborah is the coeditor and copublisher of *Bold Ink: Collected Voices of Women and Girls,* an anthology by WriteGirl, a nonprofit creative-writing organization that matches women writers with teen girls for one-on-one mentoring. She is one of WriteGirl's founding staff members and currently sits on its Board of Advisors. Deborah's first nonfiction book, *Run for Your Life: A Book for Beginning Women Runners,* is a self-help book with the goal of making the sport of running accessible to women of all abilities.

Prior to becoming a full-time writer and consultant, Deborah worked in children's television, developing original programming for Cartoon Network, managing ancillary projects for *Blue's Clues* (Nickelodeon), and producing an international campaign championing children's rights for UNICEF. While at *Blue's Clues,* she wrote more than a dozen *Blue's Clues* books, including two *New York Times* best-sellers, and coauthored a line of educational workbooks. She has produced several documentaries, including *Drawing Insight* and *Seven Days in Somalia,* and consults with companies like Nickelodeon, Disney Channel, McGraw-Hill and Offramp Films.

Deborah leads writing and creative workshops for teens, most recently participating in Mind on the Media's annual conference, *Turn Beauty Inside Out.* She has been an invited panelist at animation festivals and a frequent guest speaker at Cal Arts, UCLA and Loyola Marymount. She has an MA in Media Studies from the New School for Social Research in New York City (1996), and a BA in Broadcast Journalism from the Pennsylvania State University (1991). She lives in Seattle with her husband, Derin, son, Asher and their dog, Baxter, where she enjoys running, hiking and gardening.

To contact Deborah, write or e-mail her at:

The Real Deal
4509 Interlake Ave. N., #281
Seattle, WA 98103
e-mail: *submissions@deborahreber.com*
www.deborahreber.com

CONTRIBUTORS

Deborah Bramwell is a high school and city college student. She hopes to one day become a veterinarian.

Anne Braton dedicated this to Krissy, Lynette and Dave. A special thanks to Ms. Cazett. In loving memory of Justine Marie.

Ariana Briski will soon be a college student who stays active in the writing community by leading the Creative Writing Club at her high school.

Andja Budincich lives in Sierra Madre, California. She enjoys reading, writing and drama.

Tawnee Calhoun is currently a sophomore at Harlem High School and has thus far been awarded the National English Award by the United States Achievement Academy. She plans to attend college and become a successful novelist.

Nidhi Chacko is studying for her 11th Standard at the Rishi Valley School in Andhra Pradesh, India. Nidhi enjoys reading, swimming and music, and her main hobby is writing poems and articles. Her ambition is to become a journalist and bring to the attention of the world the miseries of the downtrodden. Please e-mail her at *nid himen@rishivalley.org*.

Matthew Chee lives in Hawaii and is currently a junior in high school. He enjoys playing tennis, writing, reading and spending time with his friends. "Just Friends" is his first published piece and is dedicated to all who have felt the blow of those two words. Matthew can be reached at *azn10sstar@yahoo.com*.

Tiffany Cheng was a member of WriteGirl, a writing organization for teenage girls. She hopes to publish as many of her writings as possible to get a head start on her goal of being a writer. If you'd like to reach her, her e-mail is *lykhunni@gmail.com.*

Fifteen-year-old **Sondra Clark** is the author of six books, including *You Can Change Your World.* She's traveled to Africa, Peru and Mexico as a spokesperson for Childcare International *(www.child care-intl.org).* Sondra loves Broadway musicals and hopes to star in "Wicked."

Raquel Dominguez is taking local college classes and plans to pursue a career in mental health. She enjoys writing poetry, reading, listening to music and spending time with friends and family. She is a good listener and people come to her for advice all the time. In her life, she plans to help teens who are going through difficult times.

Veronica Engler is a fourteen-year-old ninth grader at Mesquite High School. She loves reading, playing piano, listening to music, Japanese manga and Krispy Kreme donuts. Veronica started writing at six years old and has had several pieces published. Sharing stories with kids around the globe is her ultimate goal.

C.C. Frick says writing poetry comes from her heart and soul. Family and friends have inspired her. She hopes to someday be able to publish a book of her own. Farming, drawing, signing, animals and many other things complete the rest of the pages in the chapters of my life.

Stephanie Garinger is headed for Drake University in Des Moines, Iowa as a freshman in 2005 and is hoping to pursue a career in writing or editing. She is an avid horseback rider, traveler and a book nerd. Stephanie is thankful for amazing friendships, with humans and horses alike.

Morgan Halvorsen is a sixteen-year-old high school junior from Potomac, Maryland. She enjoys reading and most particularly writing. She aspires to become an author, providing it is a lucrative field by the time she is an adult.

Jalesa Harper is a sophomore at Norcross High School in Georgia. She enjoys reading, acting, writing, music and dance. When she completes college, she would like to be a paleontologist.

Stephanie Ives is entering her final year at North Dundas District High School. She lives in Winchester, Ontario, and after high school she wants to go to university to teach high school history because history is her passion. She loves nature, literature, sports of almost any kind, history, politics and chocolate.

Nikki Kremer, age thirteen, is an eighth-grader at Landisville Middle School in Lancaster, Pennsylvania. Previously, she has had her poetry published in *Celebrate! Young Poets Speak Out*, Pennsylvania, Fall 2004. Nikki also plays on her school field hockey and soccer teams, is active in her youth group at church and is a very busy babysitter. She and Laura remain very close friends. Nikki can be reached at *j_kremer@msn.com*.

Joel Kristenson, soon to be a high school junior, loves to take life easy, play basketball, soccer, and golf, but mostly snowboard and skateboard. He plans to attend college in the mountains and pursue an unknown career. In the summer he builds houses, swims in Lake Superior and goes camping.

Crystal Mendoza is an eleven-year-old sixth-grader who likes to read, write, play sports and listen to rap. She has been writing for two years, and has dreams of becoming a well-known children's author.

Erin Merryn is a student at Western Illinois University, studying social work and journalism. She is the author of *Stolen Innocence,* a memoir. She enjoys working with children, skiing in Colorado and spending her summers in Lake Geneva, Wisconsin. She is currently working on her second book. Please e-mail her at: *stolen_innocence 2004@yahoo.com*.

Sara Moulton is currently pursuing a Bachelor of Arts in Literature from the Richard Stockton College of New Jersey. She lives in southern New Jersey, where she is a part time lifeguard. Sara enjoys watching movies, reading, swimming and writing poetry. She hopes to complete a book of poetry before she finishes college.

Rosie Ojeda is a sophmore at California State University Channel Islands. When Rosie has free time, she enjoys surfing, going to the beach, shopping, and spending time with friends and family.

Mandy Pike is heading off to Carleton University in Ottawa in September. She loves volunteering and working with children, especially children with special needs and disabilities. She spent the summer of 2005 working at Easter Seals Camp Merrywood. Mandy loves to read, write, play guitar, play sports, coach, volunteer and work with children. Please e-mail her at *mandypike@hotmail. com*.

Chelsea Preas is a senior at Lake View High School in San Angelo, Texas. She loves playing guitar, listening to music, watching movies and talking with her friends. She plans to attend a university in Texas and major or minor in English.

Debbi Rotkowitz is currently a student at Hampshire College in Amherst, Massachusetts. She is studying theatre, photography and American Sign Language. Please contact her at *Debbi827@aol.com*.

Liia Rudolph is a senior at Strath Haven in Wallington, Pennsylvania. She loves to sing, write, act and also play and work with children. She teaches swimming and drama at a summer camp. She hopes to go to college somewhere warm and inspirational. To contact Liia, e-mail her at *liiamaicr@yahoo.com*.

Rebecca Ruiter is now a high school senior in Guelph, Ontario, looking to be a youth worker when she gets older. She loves children and volunteering around the community. Rebecca enjoys reading, writing, swimming, camping, skiing and being with friends.

Erin Shea is a thirteen-year-old girl attending Mount Pearl Intermediate School. She is currently in the eighth grade, studying both English and French. Erin enjoys writing, reading, basketball and hanging out with friends. Erin writes poetry and short stories and hopes to be a writer someday.

Jennifer Traylor graduated from North Bend High School in North Bend, Oregon, in 2005. Her future plans are to attend Linfield College in McMinnville, Oregon, to pursue a degree in premedicine. She enjoys spending time with friends and family, participating on the track team, and traveling.

Omenka Uchendu is a sophomore at Groves High School, Beverly Hills, Michigan and takes great pride in excelling at academics, sports and her writing. She also enjoys reading, relaxing with friends, and family and fashion design. She believes that with God anything is possible. E-mail her at *uche2030@yahoo.com*.

Lovely Umayam is your typical eccentric senior living in sunny California who enjoys writing poetry, performing at open-mics, kickboxing and taking random pictures with polaroids. She's currently a writer and CNN anchor in the making and is planning to travel the world. She misses Gladys very much. E-mail: *pnaigotstylez@aol.com.*

Kaleigh Vance, age fourteen, lives in Kentucky. She likes reading, playing with her pets (Luke and Sparky) and riding horses. Kaleigh enjoys writing and plans on authoring more short stories in the future. She will be a freshman in high school in August.

Alicia Vasquez is currently attending Cal Poly Pomona where she majors in sociology with an emphasis in social work and a minor in criminology. She enjoys writing poems, snowboarding and spending time with her friends. She plans to become a social worker in the future.

Clara Waddell is a future junior of Cook County High School in Grand Marais, Minnesota. Clara participates in basketball, soccer and softball. Clara loves living in a rural environment, and it is a great inspiration for her writing. She plans on going into the writing field.

Michael Wassmer began writing personal essays when he was eleven years old and hasn't stopped since. He currently attends high school and plans to graduate in 2008. What comes after that is anyone's guess, he says. Please e-mail him at *MJWassmer@hotmail.com.*

Dallas Woodburn is a freshman at USC, majoring in creative writing. Her writing credits include the magazines *Family Circle, Writer's Digest* and *Justine,* and the books *So, You Wanna Be a Writer?, Chicken Soup for the Teenage Soul IV* and *Chicken Soup for the Teenage Soul's The Real Deal: School.* Visit her Web site at *www.zest.net/writeon.*

Andrew Woods attends Philips-Osceola Area High School in central Pennsylvania. He enjoys reading, writing stories and music. He is unsure what his future plans have in store for him.

Ruth Young was on the Girls Editorial Board of *New Moon Magazine* from the time she was eleven through fourteen years of age. Her hobbies include writing, cooking, observing people and traveling. Among other things, she hopes to become an accomplished writer of some sort.

Alex Zuber is fourteen years old and is about to begin her freshman year in high school. She began writing in a secret journal when she was nine years old and has continued to write stories, personal thoughts and poems in it. Her favorite things to do are shop and hang out with her friends. In the future she hopes to become a psychologist.

PERMISSIONS

The First Day. Reprinted by permission of Clara Rose Waddell and Larry O'Brien Waddell. ©2005 Clara Rose Waddell.

Friendship Soup. Reprinted by permission of Omenka Helen Uchendu and Uche Uchendu. ©2005 Omenka Helen Uchendu.

Dear Friend. Reprinted by permission of Andja Milena Budincich and Catherine Budincich. ©2005 Andja Milena Budincich.

Being a Friend. Reprinted by permission of Rosie Ojeda. ©2005 Rosie Ojeda.

The Gardener. Reprinted by permission of Joel Kristenson and Joni Kristenson. ©2005 Joel Kristenson.

Crossing the Fence. Reprinted by permission of Omenka Helen Uchendu and Uche Uchendu. ©2005 Omenka Helen Uchendu.

A Volunteer from the Audience. Reprinted by permission of Veronica Anne Engler and Nancy Engler. ©2005 Veronica Anne Engler.

Not Really a Friend. Reprinted by permission of Tawnee Calhoun and Mary Manring. ©2005 Tawnee Calhoun.

The In-Crowd. Reprinted by permission of Tiffany Cheng and Edwin Cheng. ©2005 Tiffany Cheng.

A Deck of Snails. Reprinted by permission of Deborah Bramwell and Lois Bramwell. ©2005 Deborah Bramwell.

Andy. Reprinted by permission of Liia Rudolph and Tom Rudolph. ©2005 Liia Rudolph.

Take Care. Reprinted by permission of Chelsea Preas and Cindy Preas. ©2005 Chelsea Preas.

True Friends. Reprinted by permission of Carlene C. Frick and Charlene Frick. ©2005 Carlene C. Frick.

My Two Best Friends. Reprinted by permission of Jalesa Lashawnda Harper and Natasha Usher. ©2005 Jalesa Lashawnda Harper.

A Different Kind of Friend. Reprinted by permission of Beth Marshall. ©2005 Beth Marshall.

The Gift of Friendship. Reprinted by permission of Jennifer Lindsay Traylor and Boni Kaye Traylor. ©2005 Jennifer Lindsay Traylor.

A Friendship Never Broken. Reprinted by permission of Nikki Ann Kremer and Cheryl M. Kremer. ©2005 Nikki Ann Kremer.

Twin. Reprinted by permission of Sara R. Moulton and Michele Schneider-Moulton. ©2005 Sara R. Moulton.

My Reflection. Reprinted by permission of Alicia Aurora Vasquez. ©2003 Alicia Aurora Vasquez.

The Friendship Cake. Reprinted by permission of Sondra Clark and Silvana Clark. ©2005 Sondra Clark.

Comfort Has Four Legs. Reprinted by permission of Stephanie Carol Garinger and Cynthia Garinger. ©2005 Stephanie Carol Garinger.

A Feline Friend. Reprinted by permission of Ruth Andrea Young and Ruthanna Young. ©2005 Ruth Andrea Young.

Cello. Reprinted by permission of Crystal Mendoza and Martha Velarde. ©2005 Crystal Mendoza.

Directory Assistance. Reprinted by permission of Michael Joseph Wassmer and William Wassmer. ©2005 Michael Joseph Wassmer.

"Friends With Benefits," Prom-Style. Reprinted by permission of Dallas Woodburn and Woody Woodburn. ©2005 Dallas Woodburn.

Get the 411

Code #2556• $12.95

Weird facts, cool graphics, fun
advice and quizzes all designed to help figure
out the REAL DEAL.

Collect them all

Code #4630 • $12.95

Code #6161 • $12.95

Inspiration
and encouragement

Also Available

Chicken Soup African American Soul
Chicken Soup Body and Soul
Chicken Soup Bride's Soul
Chicken Soup Caregiver's Soul
Chicken Soup Cat and Dog Lover's Soul
Chicken Soup Christian Family Soul
Chicken Soup Christian Soul
Chicken Soup College Soul
Chicken Soup Country Soul
Chicken Soup Couple's Soul
Chicken Soup Expectant Mother's Soul
Chicken Soup Father's Soul
Chicken Soup Fisherman's Soul
Chicken Soup Girlfriend's Soul
Chicken Soup Golden Soul
Chicken Soup Golfer's Soul, Vol. I, II
Chicken Soup Horse Lover's Soul
Chicken Soup Inspire a Woman's Soul
Chicken Soup Kid's Soul
Chicken Soup Mother's Soul, Vol. I, II
Chicken Soup Nature Lover's Soul
Chicken Soup Parent's Soul
Chicken Soup Pet Lover's Soul
Chicken Soup Preteen Soul, Vol. I, II
Chicken Soup Single's Soul
Chicken Soup Soul, Vol. I-VI
Chicken Soup at Work
Chicken Soup Sports Fan's Soul
Chicken Soup Teenage Soul, Vol. I-IV
Chicken Soup Woman's Soul, Vol. I, II